Cycle Maryland

Other Guides by Bryan MacKay
Hike Maryland
Paddle Maryland

Cycle
MARYLAND

A GUIDE to Bike Paths and Rail Trails

Bryan MacKay

Photographs by Debi and Bryan MacKay

Maps by Bill Nelson

JOHNS HOPKINS UNIVERSITY PRESS · BALTIMORE

Johns Hopkins University Press
2715 North Charles Street
Baltimore, Maryland 21218-4363
www.press.jhu.edu

Library of Congress Cataloging-in-Publication Data

Names: MacKay, Bryan, author.
Title: Cycle Maryland : A Guide to Bike Paths and Rail Trails /
   Bryan MacKay ; Photographs by Debi and Bryan MacKay ; Maps by Bill Nelson.
Description: Baltimore, Maryland : Johns Hopkins University Press, 2018. |
   Includes index.
Identifiers: LCCN 2017030362| ISBN 9781421425009 (pbk. : alk. paper) |
   ISBN 1421425009 (pbk. : alk. paper) | ISBN 9781421425016 (electronic) |
   ISBN 1421425017 (electronic)
Subjects: LCSH: Bicycle touring—Maryland—Guidebooks. | Bicycle trails—
   Maryland—Guidebooks. | Rail-trails—Maryland—Guidebooks. |
   Maryland—Guidebooks.
Classification: LCC GV1045.5.M3 M34 2018 | DDC 796.609752—dc23
   LC record available at https://lccn.loc.gov/2017030362

A catalog record for this book is available from the British Library.

*Special discounts are available for bulk purchases of this book. For more information,
please contact Special Sales at specialsales@press.jh.edu.*

Contents

Preface

Welcome to *Cycle Maryland*. The last twenty years have seen a marked increase in the construction of off-road, asphalt-paved, multi-use recreational trails. Whatever name you give them, they provide the advantage of cycling without having to worry about motor vehicles—an obvious benefit when biking, especially for children. I believe a good guidebook to these recreational trails is needed, and I personally enjoy cycling these trails; these are two major reasons why I wrote this book.

Most people who cycle appreciate the considerable health benefits of this enticing physical activity. Make no mistake, cycling increases fitness, builds muscle, improves cardiovascular capacity, and even enhances your mental and emotional outlook. But in addition, many people who ride on recreational trails typically enjoy the opportunity to observe nature along the way. Whether that is seeing the first leaves as they begin to bud out, savoring prime fall color, or looking for birds, flowers, or butterflies, Maryland's recreational trails offer excellent opportunities. Some pass through unusual landscapes or unique habitats. A few even go by monuments to major historical events. Such places merit greater recognition and deserve a wider appreciation by the public for their value for conservation, education, and the quality of our shared life as Maryland citizens. I've been an educator for almost forty years, focusing on nature, ecology, and plant biology, so writing about such topics is my mission in life.

In choosing the rides for this book, I had several criteria in mind. First, I included only recreational trails longer than five contiguous miles, a distance sufficient to make loading up the bikes and driving to the trail worthwhile. Second, I included some venues that are not strictly recreation trails but are on lightly traveled roads with posted speed limits less than 25 miles per hour. Such places include Blackwater National Wildlife Refuge, Patuxent National Wildlife Refuge, the National Arboretum, and Antietam National Battlefield. These are wonderful cycling trips, and I have never felt concerned about traffic at any of these sites. Third, I included a few recreational trails that are *not* paved, including the Northern Central Railroad Trail, the Great Allegheny Passage, and the C&O Canal towpath. Recreational trails are so popular that more are being designed and built annually.

Although I tried to be comprehensive, it is probable that by the time you buy this book, a few more trails will be open for riding. I consider that a cause for celebration.

And yes, in case you're wondering, I've ridden every mile described in this book. Some places, like Patapsco Valley State Park, near my home, I've cycled several hundred times over the last half century.

The trip description for each ride includes directions and points of interest you'll encounter along the way. In addition, the text is designed to illuminate those aspects of nature you are likely to observe on your ride. Wildflowers, insects, trees, birds, and mammals are all mentioned, often within the context of their role in the ecosystem. Since you can cover more miles on a bike than while hiking, you'll have the chance to see more wildlife and the opportunity to see how the landscape changes with distance. Accompanying each trip description is a nature essay that considers a relevant organism or related concept in greater detail. Having taught ecology for more than three decades, I have found that many people are curious about the natural world around them and appreciate these short essays.

Written directions at the end of each trip description will get you to the trailhead from the Washington-Baltimore metropolitan area. A street address is included (where a useable one exists), as are GPS coordinates for the trailhead. Note that cell phone coverage is spotty in the more rural parts of Maryland, especially in the mountains (but it's a good idea to carry a fully charged cell phone nevertheless).

The paved recreational trails in this book are all officially "multiuse" trails. You will encounter many walkers, children in strollers, dogs on leashes, inline skaters, equestrians, and people in wheelchairs. Please be courteous when you ride: give warning in advance of your presence or intention to pass with the ring of a bell or a spoken word; yield right-of-way to both pedestrians and equestrians; and keep your speed under 15 miles per hour. A cheery word to other trail users is often appreciated. Remember, recreational trails are a shared public resource; treat the neighbors you encounter here as you would wish to be treated yourself. It takes a united community of trail users to tell our legislators and government officials that we all value recreational trails and that we want more to be built in the future.

I hope you enjoy using this book as you explore Maryland on your bike. May you have many safe and memorable experiences in your journeys.

Acknowledgments

The advent of off-road recreational trails rejuvenated my interest in cycling, and I am grateful to the county and state government agencies that have spent substantial amounts of public money to purchase rights-of-way and construct rideable surfaces for these trails. Thanks to Steve Carr of the Maryland Department of Natural Resources for information about several of the trails developed by that agency and included in this book.

My wife, Debi MacKay, accompanied me on most of the exploratory rides done for this book. She actually enjoyed my frequent stops to take notes and check the map and was often a willing model cyclist for photographs. Debi always carries her camera, and some of her photographs of nature grace these page. Thank you! Carl and Cathy Weber first provided me with information about the Washington, Baltimore, and Annapolis Trail, and Dave Eisenmann answered my questions about the Sligo Creek Trail. Tricia Precht and Kathy Halle accompanied me on rides on the Northern Central Railroad Trail years ago.

In 1992, a (fairly) young and definitely naïve version of me first approached Johns Hopkins University Press regarding possible publication of a guidebook to venues for hiking, cycling, and canoeing in Maryland. I am indebted to the Press, and my long-time editor, Bob Brugger, for immediately accepting the manuscript and shepherding it through publication and sales. To date, that book has sold more than 21,000 copies, and it has been gratifying to receive so many compliments on it from people who love the outdoors. Now that book about the best places in Maryland to go hiking, cycling, and paddling has received a fresh interpretation from the Press with the publication of three separate guidebooks, each devoted exclusively to a single sport. Each venue has been revisited, viewed with a clear eye, and the text revised. New sites have been added. Information about nature has been updated. I believe these new books improve significantly on the older one. I have written the book I want to grab when I leave the house for a day of safe, off-road cycling on one of Maryland's recreational trails. I appreciate my present editor at the Press, Catherine Goldstead, for her vision about this project and her steady hand at guiding it to fruition. I am also grateful to Mary Lou Kenney at the Press for her copyediting expertise.

Maps for this book have been prepared by Bill Nelson of Bill Nelson Maps: I thank him for his expertise.

While any author receives and appreciates help with a writing project, he is ultimately responsible for any errors and omissions. Should you find any you wish to tell me about, I can be contacted through Johns Hopkins University Press.

Cycling Trails in Maryland

As a child, the gift of an "English racer" bicycle soon became more to me than just another toy. I quickly realized that a bike opened up new sights and additional places to go, a wider realm of experience than could be achieved merely by walking. That bike was the epitome of freedom to a nine-year-old boy—my first opportunity to venture away from parental oversight, to ride fast with the wind in my hair, to experience the exhilaration of speed and movement. I suspect that feeling of new-found freedom is shared by almost every preteen cyclist in America, then and now.

By the mid-1970s, with a full-time job, I became a weekend warrior, riding for fun and exercise on the rural roads of the Patapsco valley and into Howard County. Meadowlarks and bluebirds were common in the grasslands and pastures I rode past, and I enjoyed stopping to watch and listen.

But change arrived. Homes began to appear in those tawny grasslands. Forests fell to housing developments. Birds and other wildlife disappeared. Most significantly, traffic became heavier; at first a nuisance, then an actual danger. For me, riding became less enjoyable. I stopped cycling.

In the early 1980s, a signal event occurred. The State of Maryland had purchased the right-of-way of the old Northern Central Railroad and begun planning for an off-road, natural surface "rail trail" running twenty miles due north from Cockeysville to the Pennsylvania line. I quickly realized this would be an ideal venue for cycling: no vehicular traffic and beautiful pastoral scenery. What a great idea.

But rail trails were a new concept in the early 1980s, and there was much opposition to the NCRT, as it was popularly known, from local landowners. Public hearings were loud and contentious. Cars parked near the trail were vandalized. Residents were afraid the trail would bring crime out of the city to their rural enclave of serenity and beauty. But the State persevered, and the trail opened to public use in 1984.

The NCRT was an immediate success. Hundreds of cyclists, walkers, runners, equestrians, and fishermen soon populated the trail from dawn to dusk. Local opposition quickly evaporated as residents realized their property values went up far faster than their taxes. Homes with access to the trail sold quickly and at a premium. Today, the NCRT (formally renamed as the Torrey C. Brown Rail Trail) is immensely popular and is recognized as one of the best rail trails in the nation. I began cycling again, primarily because of how pleasant it was to ride on the NCRT, and I ride there still.

With the advent of off-road recreational trails like the NCRT, cycling suddenly gained a much larger constituency, and one composed of citizens who were not previously cycling advocates. In particular, recreational trails permitted families with young children to participate in a healthful activity that, because of safety concerns, had previously been impossible. This sparked significant innovation in the cycling industry: well-engineered, multi-bike racks that attached to bumpers, hitches, and pickup beds; sturdy, comfortable trailers for those too young to ride themselves; and safer alternatives to training wheels for children just learning to balance and ride. Bikes for adults soon became more comfortable and sturdy as manufacturers carried over ideas learned from building mountain bikes to more recreationally oriented bikes. The State, counties, and municipalities soon began to look for other sites that might support such trails. The public demanded it, and local businesses realized such trails were economic engines. The only limitation was cost; recreational trails, whether paved or surfaced with natural materials like crushed limestone, are expensive to construct. As of this writing, there are dozens of off-road, multi-use recreational trails in Maryland. Those longer than five miles are detailed in this book. Visit any one of them and you'll find a superb cycling adventure coupled with the opportunity to experience nature in some of Maryland's most beautiful places. Enjoy!

Cycle Maryland

Assateague Island Bike Trail

Section: National Seashore Visitor Center parking lot to terminus and return
County: Worcester
Distance: 9.5 miles as described; out-and-back ride
Type: Designated roadside bike trail
Surface: Asphalt
Difficulty: Easy. Flat, but with one steep "hill" (Verrazano Bridge)
Hazards: Traffic on adjacent road, biting insects
Highlights: Barrier island, salt marsh, horses, birds
More Information: Assateague State Park, http://dnr.maryland.gov
/publiclands/Pages/eastern/assateague.aspx, (410) 641-2120.
Assateague Island National Seashore, https://nps.gov/asis/index.htm,
(410) 641-1441
Street Address: 11800 Marsh View Lane, Berlin, Maryland 21811
(Visitor Center)
GPS Coordinates: 38.247620, 75.154472 (Visitor Center)

The barrier islands on Maryland's Atlantic coast are some of the most beautiful and appealing places in the state. Fenwick Island, on which Ocean City is located, becomes the second largest city in Maryland on prime weekends like Memorial Day, July Fourth, and Labor Day. Just to the south, separated by a narrow inlet, is Assateague Island, considerably less populated but only slightly less popular. The conjunction of land and sea at places like these attracts us and has a calming, restorative effect on the human psyche.

In large measure, it is the ocean beach that draws people. But on a natural barrier island like Assateague, the beach is just one of several distinct habitat types, each with its own characteristic flora

1

and fauna. The dunes, shrub zone, maritime forest, and hypersaline marshes are all equally interesting, although conditions may make them less accessible. Fortunately, the National Park Service has helped by establishing interpretive walking trails through each life zone on Assateague, linked by a pleasant paved bike path. Cyclists will find this trip to be a fine opportunity to explore the "other" Assateague: the land behind the dunes.

This bike trail is 9.5 miles in length when ridden as described. Part of it is a separate, paved lane that runs adjacent to the park road and is separated from it by a few feet of gravel. This portion of the bike path is only wide enough for one bicycle, so it must be ridden in single file. Other parts of the trail share lightly traveled park roads with cars, but the speed limit is low enough that cyclists will not feel uncomfortable.

Trip Description

Begin your tour from the National Seashore Visitor Center parking lot located just before the Verrazano Bridge that leads onto Assateague Island. The National Seashore Visitor Center has drinking water and restroom facilities as well as information and displays. On the opposite side of the road, the State of Maryland has a lot used primarily to park boat trailers, but it is open to anyone if the National Park lot is full. You will find drinking water and restrooms here as well. Mount your bike and ride east on the dedicated paved bike path, which immediately rises steeply to the top of the Verrazano Bridge leading to Assateague Island. Named for the Italian explorer who may have stopped near here in 1524, it is the highest point for miles around and is a fine place to get an overview of the island and surrounding bays.

To the south, all the life zones of this barrier island are visible: beach, dune, shrub zone, maritime forest, salt marsh, and back bay. The tang of salt air and the earthy scent of marsh bombard your nose. Overhead, gulls and terns wheel and squawk in every season. The fecundity of life in this special place is wonderfully evident. Coast down onto the island, passing tidal guts and low marshes where Assateague's famous ponies frequently graze. Eventually the bike path bears right, where it continues parallel to Bayberry Drive in a southerly direction.

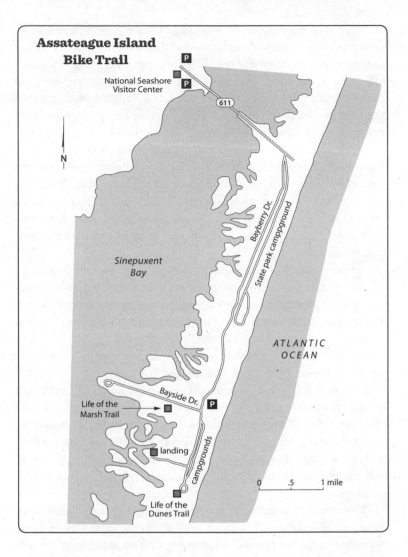

**Assateague Island
Bike Trail**

National Seashore
Visitor Center

611

Bayberry Dr.

State park campground

Sinepuxent
Bay

ATLANTIC
OCEAN

Bayside Dr.

Life of the
Marsh Trail

landing

campgrounds

0   .5   1 mile

Life of the
Dunes Trail

N

The bike path traverses the shrub zone of Assateague Island. Thus a dense hedge of vegetation dominated by fragrant bayberry, wax myrtle, common reed, cattail, loblolly pine, and poison ivy encroaches on the bayward (western) side. Bird life is abundant; you are likely to see catbirds, various sparrows, and yellow warblers in the woody vegetation and red-winged blackbirds in the reeds. Insect life abounds as well; if the day is without a breeze, don't dawdle or the mosquitoes will attack in droves.

Pass the campgrounds of Assateague State Park, which occupy the area on the ocean side of the road and bike path. The feral horses of Assateague are often sighted in this campground. While they usually graze on the low vegetation, they are not above raiding any food inadvertently left out by campers. After two miles, management of the land passes to the National Park Service and you are actually riding in Assateague Island National Seashore. Go another half mile and turn right onto Bayside Drive. Although this road has no official bike path and no shoulders, it is lightly traveled, and all but the youngest riders should not mind the traffic. A short distance down Bayside Drive is the parking lot for the Life of the Marsh nature trail. This is a good opportunity to see some of the prettiest natural habitats on Assateague, so lock your bike and walk to the trail entrance.

A boardwalk leads through the wall of vegetation and out onto the salt marsh. This enables visitors to see the life of this most interesting habitat without the difficulties normally involved: slippery, smelly mud underfoot and clouds of mosquitoes rising to your epidermis for a prospective blood meal.

A salt marsh is a place of transition, where land and sea meet, yet it is different from either. Washed by high tides twice a day, the plants and animals that live here are exposed to hours of inundation by salty water that pulls precious fresh water from living tissues. At low tide, sun and wind cook and desiccate, imposing a whole new set of stresses. In spite of these extreme conditions, many organisms have adapted to this harsh and beautiful environment. Indeed, salt marshes are the most productive natural habitat found on earth today.

The marsh at Assateague is dominated by saltmarsh cordgrass, *Spartina alterniflora*. This tough, resilient grass covers many acres surrounding the boardwalk and gives the first impression of a neatly kept lawn. It is one of only a few species of higher plant that can tolerate the twice-daily tidal cycle of flooding and desiccation and, therefore, much of the low marsh is a monoculture of cordgrass. Cordgrass exhibits several adaptations that allow it to live in salty water. Like dunegrass, cordgrass can secrete salt through special cells along the blade. In the early morning light, these crystals of salt may glitter like jewels scattered across the marsh. The roots of cordgrass can filter out fresh water from the salty bay water.

Despite the stresses with which they must deal, plants living in a salt marsh enjoy certain advantages. Each high tide brings a fresh supply of nutrients and oxygen to the cordgrass, and light and competition from other plant species are never limiting factors. Cordgrass spreads aggressively by means of underground rhizomes that form a thick, dense mass. This root system filters out sediments from seawater and thus builds up the marsh. In fact plantings of cordgrass have been successful in controlling erosion along some shorelines in Chesapeake Bay.

Cordgrass plays a dominant role in the ecology of Sinepuxent Bay, the hypersaline embayment behind Assateague Island. Dead plant material is broken down into detritus by the actions of bacteria, waves, and microscopic grazing animals. About half of this detritus stays in the marsh and acts as a food source for marshland inhabitants, while the other half is washed into the bay. Here it forms the basis for an aquatic food chain, being consumed by mussels, clams, oysters, molluscs, and other creatures. Cordgrass also provides shelter and protection to immature and small adult fish, shrimp, crabs, and snails.

The area traversed by this boardwalk was dredged and drained in the 1950s to be made into a marina as part of the grandiose development schemes for Assateague Island. The devastating storm of 1962 dashed these hopes, however, and the island was purchased by the federal government in 1965. Fifty years later, evidence of ditching for mosquito control, spoil banks where fill dirt was dumped during construction, and dredging for boat slips still mar the landscape.

An arm of the boardwalk leads to an observation platform. From this slight but significant elevation, the wide expanse of Sinepuxent Bay and surrounding marshes spreads for miles. This is a good place to look for birds. Laughing gulls and common terns are frequently seen diving for fish in warm weather. Overhead, snowy egrets, glossy ibis, and various gulls glide by. Willets feed in the marshes, their wings flashing a black and white pattern as they fly.

The boardwalk trail leads down to the water's edge and a tiny white sand beach. Windrows of eelgrass have been tossed up to the high tide line, where beach fleas, flies, and other insects forage through the decaying vegetation. Eelgrass is a submerged aquatic flowering plant that covers extensive areas of the floor of Sinepuxent Bay. Like dunegrass on the beach and cordgrass in the marsh, eelgrass is a keystone species for the aquatic community, providing a protected habitat for numerous animal species and stabilizing bottom sediments and dampening wave action. It contributes to the food chain both indirectly by acting as a substrate for algal growth and directly when it dies back each winter. Small patches of eelgrass growing on the bottom may be seen in the shallow water just offshore; more extensive seagrass meadows lie farther out in deeper water.

Many visitors to the Life of the Marsh Trail are content merely to observe from the boardwalk. However, there is no better way to really appreciate the marshes and back bays of Assateague than to wade right in and become a part of them. So roll up your pants legs, kick off your shoes, and step into the water. This little semi-enclosed bay of a few hundred yards' diameter is ideal for a fluvial walk because it is shallow and not too muddy.

Taste the water of Sinepuxent Bay. Seawater is very salty to the taste and measures about 33 parts salt per thousand parts water, with little variation. Here in the back bays, however, a series of sunny, calm days may evaporate so much water (leaving the salt molecules behind) that salinity rises to as high as 40 parts per thousand. Because the whole bay is so shallow (typically less than four feet deep at low tide) and connections to the ocean are so few, bay water does not get mixed with ocean water, and it becomes so hypersaline that one can taste the difference.

As you slosh along the shore, all sorts of small aquatic animals will scurry away. These creatures can be easily captured and examined by running a seine net, available from stores that sell fishing equipment. In such shallow waters, a typical pass along 50 feet of shoreline will yield hundreds of animals. Most common will be small fish, especially members of the minnow family like killifish and mummichogs. Grass shrimp, transparent crustaceans about an inch long, will be equally plentiful. Immature blue crabs sheltering in patches of eelgrass sometimes show up, but most are too quick to be trapped by the seine.

A visit in late May or early June will most likely yield a few horseshoe crabs cruising the shallows. These primitive arthropods evolved more than 200 million years ago in shallow warm seas and have flourished unchanged ever since. With a hard brown carapace averaging about a foot in diameter and a nasty-looking

Verrazano Bridge and dedicated bike path

(but harmless) spike protruding from the rear, horseshoe crabs patrol the bay and ocean bottoms for clams and worms. In late May, horseshoe crabs migrate to the beaches of lower Delaware Bay to breed, resulting in one of the truly impressive wildlife spectacles in North America. Although Delaware Bay is the epicenter of breeding activity, some also occurs on more distant beaches, such as those at Assateague.

Explore as much of this little bay as you care to and then return to the boardwalk. The path passes through another screen of dense vegetation at the edge of the marsh and ends at the parking lot.

Remounting your bike, continue west on Bayside Drive. The road ends at a picnic area on an exposed peninsula of land where conditions are almost always windy. For this reason, it is a popular area for windsurfers, and their colorful sailboards are frequently seen darting back and forth across Sinepuxent Bay. Clamming is allowed here, although beds near the shore become depleted rather early in the season.

Pedal back up Bayside Drive to Bayberry Drive, turning right to continue your ride south on the island. Within 100 yards, the bike path leaves Bayberry Drive by bearing left into the even more lightly traveled campground access road. If you like wildflowers, check the grassy wet swales in the campground itself; blue-eyed grass and blue toadflax abound in spring, and summer brings on meadow beauties and ladies' tresses orchids. Purple gerardias are common in the fall. The bike trail terminates 0.6 mile farther on at the Life of the Dunes nature trail. Once again, park and lock your bike.

This trail is a short loop through the secondary dune and shrub habitats. Although it is interesting, be forewarned: unless there is a strong breeze, the mosquitoes could well be intolerable between May and October. A number of factors interact to determine how bad the level of mosquitoes will be on Assateague, including time of year, wind speed and direction, and rainfall. If the island has undergone a long dry period, the mosquito population may not be too large, but wet weather usually results in an unpleasant experience with Assateague's most numerous species.

The trail winds through the secondary dunes, where expanses of bare sand alternate with hillocks of vegetation. Plants that colonize bare sand are true pioneers, especially adapted to life in a hot, dry, nutrient-poor environment. Most of them have deep-delving, extensive root systems, a dense, bushlike structure, and leaves modified by waxy cuticles, scales, or dense hairs. The most common of these plants is beach heather, a low, spreading shrubby plant with scalelike leaves. In dry periods, it may appear dead, but a good rain will restore it to green health. Beach heather is quite beautiful in May, when it bears many tiny yellow flowers.

As plants like beach heather and dunegrass grow and expand, they modify the habitat by building soil, preserving soil moisture, serving as windbreaks, and increasing local humidity. This modification in turn allows other plants to colonize, including shrubs like bayberry, wax myrtle, and winged sumac and vines like poison ivy and muscadine grape.

As the trail winds farther back into the secondary dunes, vegetation becomes more lush, and most of the bare sand is covered. Small trees, such as beach plum, black cherry, sassafrass, and a few oaks appear; these provide food for island animals. Most of these specimens are short because the salt spray kills the tender growing buds at the crowns of trees. Instead of growing vertically, these trees tend to spread outward as they grow.

This scrubby habitat is excellent for birding, and catbirds, quail, towhees, cardinals, and robins are common. Raccoons and foxes are surprisingly plentiful on Assateague, and this is the best habitat in which to encounter them (usually at dawn or dusk, when you're alone and quiet). The diversity of insects of all types increases dramatically in the denser vegetation.

The Life of the Dunes Trail eventually loops back to the start after a walk of less than half a mile. Remount your bike and return to your car via the bike path.

Directions

From Baltimore or Washington, cross the Bay Bridge and continue south on Route 50 through Easton, Cambridge, and Salisbury. Just before the bridge to Ocean City, turn right on Route 611 at the prominent sign marking Assateague Island National Seashore. Follow Route 611 for about five miles. Park in the National Seashore Visitor Center lot. If this lot is full, park in the marina lot across Route 611.

Other Outdoor Recreational Opportunities Nearby

Camping facilities are available at both the state park and the national seashore. The state park has hot-water showers and flush toilets; it is so popular that reservations are a must. The national seashore sites have only portable toilets and cold-water showers. In hot weather, a screen house is a virtual necessity at both campgrounds, providing refuge from the sun and bugs.

The beach is a great place to walk, and there are more than thirty miles of public beach on Assateague. Hike north, toward Ocean City, if you prefer solitude.

Canoes and kayaks can be rented seasonally from the Old Ferry Landing at Assateague Island National Seashore. Stay close to shore; the prevailing breeze from the south almost always keeps Sinepuxent Bay choppy, and paddling is difficult in the open waters. You'll find more to see in the winding tidal guts anyway.

ASSATEAGUE PONIES

If there is one species that the public associates with Assateague Island it is the feral ponies that have long been a part of the life and lore of Maryland's only natural barrier island. Legend has it that Assateague ponies are the descendants of the survivors of a shipwrecked seventeenth-century Spanish galleon. There is, however, no evidence that this romantic tale is true; the facts are far more pedestrian. Early colonists grazed their horses on Assateague because no fences were required and natural forage was sufficient if not abundant.

There are two distinct pony herds on Assateague, separated by a fence crossing the island from ocean to bay at the Maryland-Virginia border. The Virginia herd is owned by the Chincoteague Volunteer Fire Company and managed with the assistance of the Chincoteague National Wildlife Refuge. Each year, excess foals are removed from the herd and sold in the famous Chincoteague "pony penning." The Maryland herd is treated as a wild population, receiving little veterinary care, forage supplements, or management.

Assateague ponies have significant effects on the native plants of the island. Large grazing animals process a great deal of vegetation, and urine and manure deposition may affect local soil and water chemistry. Visible effects of grazing and trampling can be seen, and may variably affect the many endemic, unusual, and endangered plant species on the island. Horses often graze the beach grass atop primary dunes, a process that accelerates erosion of the island's main protection against storm damage. Ponies are also inveterate foragers, as campers who leave food unattended or tents unzipped often discover. Yet despite these negative effects, the ponies remain an intrinsic part of the Assateague experience.

Since 1987, the National Park Service herd has been controlled with a vaccine that prevents pregnancy. This proved highly effective; only one out of the 26 mares treated foaled in that first year. In addition to being relatively inexpensive, effective, and reversible, this method did not affect pregnancies already in progress, did not affect pony behavior, and did not stress animals as do techniques requiring capture and surgery. This represented the first successful application of the technique of immunocontraception to uncaptured, free-roaming wild animals.

The contraception program at Assateague, now almost thirty years old as of this writing (2017), has at last reached a tipping point. The pony population, which held steady for many years at about 140 animals, has now dropped to 88, largely due to natural causes like old age and illness. As many as half the mares have reached an age where they will no longer foal. If the contraception program were to continue, demographics imply the herd would drop well below its target level of 80–100 horses. For this reason, no horses will be given contraception in 2017, and in future years contraception can be adjusted to result in a pony herd of optimum size.

Blackwater National Wildlife Refuge

Section: Wildlife Refuge circuit
County: Dorchester
Distance: 7.5 miles as described; circuit ride
Type: Refuge roads and lightly traveled public roads
Surface: Asphalt
Difficulty: Easy. Flat
Hazards: Light vehicular traffic
Highlights: Salt marsh, waterfowl, bald eagles, and other birds
More Information: Blackwater National Wildlife Refuge, https://fws.gov
   /refuge/Blackwater, (410) 228-2677
Street Address: Near 2145 Key Wallace Drive, Cambridge, Maryland 21613
GPS Coordinates: 38.444829, 76.119511 (Visitor Center)

More Marylanders have been introduced to birdwatching at Blackwater National Wildlife Refuge than at any other single location. No matter whom you talk to in Washington or Baltimore, he or she has probably visited Blackwater, or at least heard of it. On any given weekend in fall and winter, cars full of casual birdwatchers and hard-core birders circle Wildlife Drive, awed by the teeming flocks of Canada geese, pleased at the glimpse of a great blue heron, and hopeful of sighting a bald eagle. Birding can be spectacularly good at Blackwater, especially for novices, and crowds don't seem to affect the birds any more than a single vehicle does. The refuge drive is open to bicycle traffic, allowing the more energetic a chance to stretch cramped legs after the two-hour drive from the western shore. Cycling the refuge also permits a more complete sensory experience: the calls and songs of birds are more easily heard, the

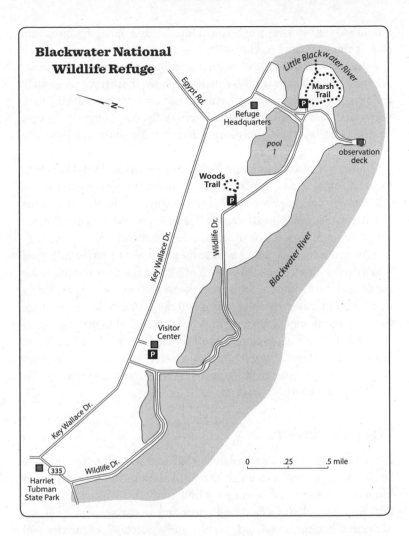

Blackwater National Wildlife Refuge

Little Blackwater River

Marsh Trail

P

Egypt Rd.

Refuge Headquarters

pool 1

observation deck

Woods Trail

P

Key Wallace Dr.

Wildlife Dr.

Blackwater River

Visitor Center

P

Key Wallace Dr.

335

Wildlife Dr.

Harriet Tubman State Park

0   .25   .5 mile

fragrance of the marsh more fully appreciable, and the full dome of the sky accessible to sight.

Blackwater exists primarily to service migratory waterfowl. Some overwinter on the fields, ponds, and marshes, taking advantage of the seeds and vegetation of managed habitats on the refuge or traveling out to nearby farms to glean waste agricultural grains. Other birds use Blackwater as a staging ground—a place where they can safely rest and fatten up for a few weeks before resuming the southward migration. For these reasons, Blackwater has its greatest abundance and diversity of birds in late fall and earliest winter, and that is the best time to visit. Choose a sunny, windless day when the thin light warms the chilly air and Blackwater can be a most pleasant place. That said, other seasons have their rewards as well. Bald eagles are common year-round, but especially so in summer, when that year's class of eaglets begin to fly. American egrets also summer on the refuge, easily located as they dot the marsh like tufts of distant cotton.

Make sure you bring along a pair of binoculars and a field guide to birds. If you have one, a spotting scope on a tripod is also useful and will make you popular with friends and strangers. At almost all sites in the United States, birds are wary and keep just outside shotgun range, so a really good look requires magnification.

The route described is a 7.5-mile loop. It is not a particularly good bike trip for children because almost half of the route is on public roads with no shoulders. However, even the public roads are fairly safe for adult riders, because almost all the traffic consists of refuge visitors intent only on birding and not interested in getting somewhere fast. Roads in the refuge itself have a 25-mph speed limit and are very safe; bicyclists typically move faster than cars. Just be alert for vehicles making sudden stops and starts, oblivious to your presence, as a new bird is sighted.

Trip Description

Begin your visit to Blackwater at the Visitor Center on Key Wallace Drive. Here you will find an auditorium showing movies, mounted birds (so you can brush up on your field marks), TV monitors showing real-time video of a bald eagle nest and an osprey nest, a census of avian inhabitants updated weekly, and a notebook of rarities and oddities observed recently. The refuge staff and volunteers on duty can answer most of your questions. Upon arrival, glance out the back window and check the dead trees standing far out in the marsh; these perches are frequented by bald eagles. If something is occupying a tree, you might want to visit the second-floor observatory, where powerful spotting scopes useful in identifying the bird in question are available. The Visitor Center has wheelchair-accessible bathrooms, drinking water, trash cans, a native plant garden, and a few picnic tables.

From the Visitor Center, cycle down the driveway to Key Wallace Drive. After the geese arrive, typically in mid-October, the adjacent fields will be full of the big honkers. Canada geese are the most common birds at Blackwater, where counts of 30,000 are not uncommon. Among the brown and black Canadas, some snow geese are usually found. These smaller birds come in two color phases: the "blue goose," with a white head and otherwise overall muddy blue coloration, and the prettier white phase, with black wing tips. There are few sights more spectacular than a flight of snows wheeling over a salt marsh, sunlight glinting off their wings, turning in unison and settling to the earth like autumn frost. There are times at Blackwater when geese darken the sky in immense flights and the world seems young and immortal.

Turn right on Key Wallace Drive. There are no shoulders, so keep to the right and use care. After 1.7 miles, turn right onto Wildlife Drive. An entry fee is charged here, even for cyclists.

Just beyond some large storage sheds, Pool 1 to your right is often filled with loafing Canada geese and a nice variety of ducks. Mallards are typically the most common, but you can almost always see pintails here as well. Key identification marks for the pintail are a conspicuous white line running from the white neck into the side of the dark head and a long needle-pointed tail. Other ducks might include the nondescript black duck, gadwall, and blue-winged teal. All of these ducks are "dabbling ducks," so named for their habit of feeding. They require shallow water for feeding since they merely invert themselves so that their rear ends point skyward as they glean seeds, grains, and insects from the pond bottom. During spring and summer, this freshwater pool is drained, and a variety of high-quality wetland plants grow to maturity. The pool is then flooded in the fall to a depth of less than a foot, killing the plants and making their seeds and stems available to ducks.

The road forks near the far end of Pool 1. Turn left and pedal to the parking lot for foot trails. Dismount, lock your bike, and take a stroll through the loblolly pine forest. Between the evergreen loblolly pines, holly, and greenbrier, it's a colorful place on a winter's day. Look for typical winter residents like chickadees, titmice, nuthatches, and various woodpeckers. At the far end of the trail, a boardwalk traverses the salt marsh to a viewing platform where you can scan the Little Blackwater River for herons, eagles, and dabbling ducks.

Return to your bike and pedal farther out this spur to its end. An elevated platform permits views over thousands of acres of marsh, mud, and water (depending on tide). From this point, it's easy to understand how Blackwater got its nickname as "the Everglades of the North." This viewing platform also allows you to look down into the surrounding cattail marsh; in late spring this wetland is home to red-winged blackbirds, marsh wrens, and hordes of winged biting insects.

Cycle back to the fork and bear left onto Wildlife Drive. The road follows the south side of Pool 1, but views over the marsh are broken by a screen of vegetation. In summer and early fall, American egrets can sometimes be seen here, before they migrate.

The road enters a mixed hardwood–loblolly pine forest and continues in this habitat for about three-quarters of a mile. Here is your best chance to sight a Delmarva fox squirrel. An officially "endangered" mammal until it was delisted in 2015, Delmarvas are almost twice as big as common gray squirrels and have a lighter pelage and more erect, foxlike ears. They prefer mature woods with an open understory, habitat conducive to their preference for running across the forest floor rather than climbing the nearest tree. At the end of this straightaway are another parking lot and trail—pleasant enough, but not too different from the rest of the forest through which you have just cycled.

The road emerges from the woods and runs westerly, built on a spoil bank dredged from the inside of the road. Thus the ditch adjacent to the road is a permanent freshwater pool, and wet agricultural lands and freshwater marsh lie beyond. More geese and ducks may be found here, and great blue herons stand sentinel at regular intervals. Northern harriers (formerly called marsh hawks) are frequently seen coursing over the land in search of prey.

On the opposite side of the road and about a mile farther along, a nesting platform stands above the marsh. This platform and others like it in more remote places in the refuge were erected for use by osprey. Thirty years ago, these fish hawks were rare in the Chesapeake Bay region, their numbers having been decimated primarily by DDT and other pesticides. Once these chemicals were banned, osprey made a dramatic comeback that was speeded by their acceptance of artificial nesting platforms. Today ospreys are common throughout the Bay. In winter, when ospreys have migrated, this platform is favored by resting bald eagles.

Wildlife Drive continues through similar habitat, with wide vistas across the marsh, for several miles. There is one fork in the road in this stretch; turn left here unless you're in a hurry to get back to the Visitor Center. Wildlife Drive ends at Route 335. Turning right, you may want to consider stopping at Harriet Tubman State Park, just across the road, where there are displays and information about the famous "conductor" on the Underground Railroad. Harriet Tubman lived and worked in the immediate area. After visiting, cycle 200 yards more on Route 355 and turn right again onto Key Wallace Drive. Return to the Visitor Center.

Most visitors to Blackwater leave home in the morning, arriving at the refuge before noon and departing a few hours later. But if you can arrange your schedule accordingly, there is no more dramatic time at Blackwater than dusk. By late fall, many of the geese go out to feed in nearby fields, returning in wave after wave at day's end. Goose music fills the air in a cacophony so loud as to render conversation impossible. Outlined against a red sunset sky, chevrons of geese make such moments unforgettable.

Directions

From Baltimore or Washington, take Route 50 over the Bay Bridge. As you leave Cambridge, turn right on Woods Road. Go 0.9 mile and turn right onto Route 16. Proceed 6.3 miles to the little crossroads of Church Creek. Turn left onto Route 335. Go 3.9 miles to Key Wallace Drive. Turn left; the Visitor Center driveway is 1.0 mile ahead on your right.

Other Outdoor Recreational Opportunities Nearby

For cyclists who don't mind riding on lightly traveled rural roads without shoulders, the refuge offers a map of a 25-mile route that circumnavigates the refuge; ask at the Visitor Center. There are also three designated paddling routes through the refuge for those with canoes or kayaks.

BALD EAGLES

Few sights in Maryland are more stirring than a mature bald eagle in flight. As it soars high overhead on a seven-foot wingspan, its size, white head, and white tail make it unmistakable. We are fortunate that our national bird is found in many parts of Maryland throughout the year. Although bald eagles are not common, your chances of seeing one are fairly good—if you know where to go.

Bald eagles are birds of the water. Their primary food is fish, snatched from near the water's surface by powerful talons, although they will feed on carrion, waterfowl, and even turtles. For this reason, they are most common along the 11,684 miles of Chesapeake Bay shoreline (including tidal tributaries). The population before the start of colonization in the seventeenth century has been estimated at 600 breeding pairs (plus a fair number of nonbreeding juveniles).

Bald eagle populations declined dramatically in the 1950s. By 1962 there were only about 65 pairs in Maryland. Worse still, those eagles that were left were experiencing severe reproductive failure. Of 37 nests observed, only 5 produced 7 young that year. Clearly the bald eagle was threatened with extinction in Maryland.

That same year, Rachel Carson published *Silent Spring*, documenting the extent of related problems with many bird species and proposing that pesticides like DDT were responsible for these declines. In the subsequent decade, she was proven correct; studies conclusively demonstrated that eggshell thinning was correlated with levels of pesticide residues, especially those of DDT and its metabolites. In the Chesapeake region, DDE levels exceeded five parts per million in eggshells, and these same shells decreased in thickness by 13 percent. This thinning weakened the eggs so much that incubating mothers often broke them. In 1967 the bald eagle was listed by the US Fish and Wildlife Service as an endangered species, both in Maryland and throughout the nation.

In an unusual example of science driving public policy, the Environmental Protection Agency (EPA) banned organochlorine pesticides, including DDT, in 1972. Within a few years, eggshells became thicker, and more young eagles were fledged. For example, in 1977, 41 pairs fledged 45 eaglets, an average of 1.1 per pair per year. In 2004, 368 pairs fledged 445 young. Not only had the breeding population size increased, but reproductive success was higher. With similar positive reports coming in from most of the bald eagle's breeding range throughout the United States, the US Fish and Wildlife Service in 2007 removed the bald eagle from the endangered species list, declaring the species "recovered." Although this downlisting does not affect the protection afforded the bald eagle, the change in status is an indication that populations of endangered species can be restored by careful management. In 2015, Chesapeake Bay hosted more than 1,500 breeding pairs of bald eagles.

Although all this is good news for bald eagles in Maryland, their future is not entirely rosy. Further expansion of the population is dependent on the availability of suitable nesting habitat, and the amount of such habitat is declining rapidly as development takes away more and more waterfront land. Since 2000,

(continued)

scientists have noted that bald eagles occasionally build a nest in a tree in the middle of a great blue heron nesting colony, presumably because trees suitable for nesting are in short supply. Bald eagles are very susceptible to human disturbance (unlike ospreys), and so require large tracts of undeveloped land. For example, a major roost site in the Chesapeake region is Aberdeen Proving Grounds, where artillery testing provides large tracts of land where humans do not venture. The birds are willing to put up with the noise in exchange for the privacy.

The recovery of the bald eagle within living memory has allowed many more people to view our national bird. Blackwater National Wildlife Refuge sheltered 207 bald eagles in winter 2015, and that number increases in the summer when immatures and newly fledged birds swell the population. The area below Conowingo Dam in Harford County is another hotspot, especially in late fall. Dozens of eagles are often in view, and some come quite close, roosting in trees above the public viewing area.

Thus, bald eagles in Maryland are doing well. We are all the richer for living in a state where we might look up to see the majestic beauty of one of these birds, wheeling overhead, sunlit against an azure sky, the symbol of a free America.

Cross Island Trail

Section: Terrapin Nature Park to Kent Narrows Public Boat Ramp
County: Queen Anne's
Distance: 5.4 miles one way
Type: Multi-use recreational trail
Surface: Asphalt
Difficulty: Easy. Virtually flat
Hazards: Road crossings
Highlights: Chesapeake Bay views, holly trees
More Information: Queen Anne's County Department of Parks and
    Recreation, (410) 758-0835
Street Address: 191 Log Canoe Circle, Stevensville, Maryland 21666
    (Terrapin Nature Park)
GPS Coordinates: 38.989530, 76.320249 (Terrapin Nature Park trailhead)

The Cross Island Trail may be seen by more people than any other multi-use trail in Maryland. That's because from the western end of the Kent Island bridge, the primary route to Ocean City, the trail's wooden boardwalk over Piney Creek is clearly visible. When traffic backs up, it's hard not to look over at happy cyclists wheeling along and wish you were one of them, free of the hassles involved in going "downee oshun."

The Cross Island Trail is not heavily used. For experienced and dedicated cyclists, its 11-mile round trip is barely enough to work up a sweat. There are a half dozen road crossings to contend with. For groups with children, or for novices, however, Cross Island is a fine ride. In addition, the two termini provide interesting destinations that couple well with cycling. At the western end, Terrapin Nature Park has two miles of foot trails traversing forest, field, marsh, and Chesapeake Bay waterfront. At the eastern terminus are the

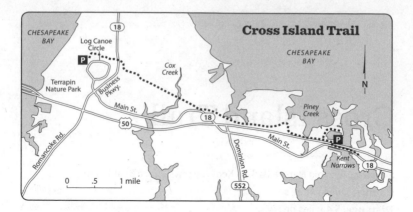

restaurants and taverns of Kent Narrows, a popular place in its own right. Take the time to visit all three, park, trail, and restaurant, and you have a recipe for a fine day out-of-doors.

Trip Description

Begin your ride from Terrapin Nature Park in Stevensville, just a mile from the eastern end of the Chesapeake Bay Bridge. There are portable toilets here but no water. Before (or after) your ride, be sure to visit the beach at this park. There are lovely views across the Bay, and the waters off the shoreline are popular with wind surfers and kite boarders. Tawny grasses and windswept trees make a dramatic scene along the beach, and there are sheltered nooks for sunbathing and picnicking. Swimming is permitted but there are no lifeguards. Inland, a variety of habitats host an assortment of butterflies and other insects, birds of brushy places, and even a few winter water-fowl on the small ponds.

The first mile of the Cross Island Trail is a pleasant ride, with a screen of trees separating the trail from the surrounding agricultural fields. While most of the trees are young, at a sharp S turn is a large willow oak, perhaps the largest in the county. Willow oaks are favored for their rapid growth, long life, and abundant annual acorn production. It is easily recognized by its fingerlike lobeless leaves that taper to a point.

Between mile 0.9 and 1.5 the trail passes through a series of athletic fields associated with Kent Island High School and Old Love

Point Park. There are several road crossings in this stretch, but most are busy only during athletic events.

At mile 2.0 the trail crosses the upper reaches of Cox Creek on a wooden bridge. Unfortunately, the marshes here are composed almost exclusively of *Phragmites*, the common reed. This non-native, invasive grass grows up to twelve feet tall and outcompetes marsh plants that are more beneficial to birds and other wildlife.

Much of the middle portion of the Cross Island Trail runs within sight of and parallel to Route 50. It can be noisy, and the shops that line this busy road detract from the pastoral scenery seen elsewhere on the trail. At mile 3.8, however, the trail enters a beautiful mature woods with tall loblolly pines and sweet gum trees overhead. What is especially notable, however, are the many American holly trees that form an understory. Many are twenty to thirty feet tall with dense dark green leaves and red berries. This is an exceptional grove of hollies that puts the cyclist in a winter holiday mindset even in summer.

Once the trail emerges from this forest, it soon crosses Piney Creek on a long wooden bridge. The view to the north is of the wide Choptank River, fringed by marsh and loblolly pine trees. It's classic Chesapeake country. Look for great blue herons, Canada geese, mallards, and perhaps a few more exotic species of ducks loafing in the sheltered coves. Once again, most of the wetland vegetation is *Phragmites*.

The trail passes a mostly abandoned outlet mall and then reaches a T intersection. Turn left to explore the boatyards and condos of Swan Cove, or turn right to continue to the Kent Narrows Public Boat Ramp, where there are many parking spaces underneath Route 50 as well as a few portable toilets. The dedicated bike trail continues over the Kent Island drawbridge, just beyond which the many seafood packing houses, restaurants, and watering holes of the Kent Narrows community may be enjoyed. Return to Terrapin Nature Park by the same route, for a total ride of 10.8 miles.

Directions

From either Washington, DC, or Baltimore, take Route 50 over the Chesapeake Bay Bridge. Take the first exit after the bridge, exit 37, turning left onto Route 8. Go 0.4 miles, turn left on Skipjack Parkway, and then left again on Log Canoe Circle. Terrapin Nature Park is 0.4 miles down Log Canoe Circle, but its sign is inconspicuous.

Other Outdoor Recreational Opportunities Nearby

Sandy Point State Park, with its beaches and marina, lies on the opposite shore of Chesapeake Bay from Terrapin Nature Park.

EXTINCTIONS IN MARYLAND

Maryland before the arrival of the white settlers almost 400 years ago was a remarkably different place than it is today. Even the best of our wild places have changed in appearance and in their biological diversity. Animals that roamed from the Chesapeake shores to the rocky wilds of the Appalachians are now missing, including some that were the biggest and most plentiful. New species, mostly invaders from other continents brought here accidentally or on purpose by humans, have become established and have had disproportional effects on native life forms. Even the kinds of trees that dominate Maryland's forested landscapes have changed.

Early white explorers and colonists were greatly impressed by the richness of Maryland. Animal life abounded, and hunters were rewarded with full larders. When the forests were cleared, the fertile soil responded with bumper crops of tobacco, grains, and vegetables. But as colonists spread to the far corners of what would later become Maryland, a number of species, mostly large mammals, were driven to extinction by overhunting. These included timber wolves, elk, wood bison, and cougars. Most were rare by the Revolution and extinct by 1850. Surprisingly, the white-tailed deer, so familiar to us now, was uncommon as well, surviving only in small populations in remote, tangled areas. Black bears were virtually eradicated in the state, although strays from viable populations in nearby Pennsylvania and West Virginia were reported almost every year. A ban on hunting permitted black bears to become reestablished in western Maryland, and now the population supports a well-regulated annual hunting season.

Bird life was rich as well. The river valleys of the southern Eastern Shore contained large numbers of Carolina parakeets, while the forested uplands harbored incredible densities of passenger pigeons during their migration. Both species are now extinct, not just in Maryland but worldwide.

The most significant extinction among the state's flora was more recent than most of the animal extinctions. Chestnut was the dominant tree species in the eastern forest, sometimes

(continued)

composing as much as 50 percent of the trees on a given site. Its annual production of mast (chestnuts) was an important food source for many forest-dwelling animals. Chestnut wood, hard and rot-resistant, was prized by farmers and foresters. Sometime in the early years of the twentieth century, a fungal parasite known as chestnut blight arrived from Asia. Quickly establishing itself in the susceptible wild populations of chestnut trees, the fungus infected the inner bark of the tree. Death followed, although the hardy roots even today send up sprouts, more than eighty years later. Unfortunately, the fungus also still lives in the roots and re-infects the tree at the sapling stage.

Although these extinctions are the most well known, there have no doubt been many others, usually of obscure, poorly studied species like fish, insects, fungi, mosses, and bacteria. Even among the flowering plants, the Department of Natural Resources lists 65 species believed to have been extirpated from Maryland. Organisms that are rare to start with may never have become known to science before going extinct. For example, the Maryland Natural Heritage Program discovered the state's first population of mountain sandwort, a small flower, in 1989. The site has now been protected from development.

Armchair naturalists like to speculate on how different the ecology of Maryland would be if we had with us the full complement of now-extinct species. Although such speculation is sheer guesswork, there is no doubt that Maryland is the poorer for the loss of its precious natural heritage. We can only dedicate ourselves to stopping future losses.

Chesapeake and Delaware Canal Trail

Section: Chesapeake City, Maryland, to Delaware City, Delaware
County: Cecil (Maryland); New Castle (Delaware)
Distance: 15.6 miles one way
Type: Multi-use recreational trail
Surface: Asphalt
Difficulty: Easy. Flat with a few short hills
Hazards: None
Highlights: Water views, really big ships
Street Address: 300 Bank Street, Chesapeake City, Maryland 21915
  (Chesapeake City trailhead)
GPS Coordinates: 39.529860, 75.810988 (Chesapeake City trailhead)

Many of our paved multi-use recreational trails follow the rights-of-way of abandoned railroads. The C&D Canal Trail is different: it follows what was once an access road for the Chesapeake and Delaware Canal, originally used only by official vehicles. As such, it runs parallel to the canal for most of its 15.6-mile length, diverging just a few times for short hills that provide interest and as the trail enters the town of Delaware City. In Maryland, the official name of the trail is the Ben Cardin Trail; in Delaware, it is the Michael Castle Trail. Cardin is presently a US Senator for Maryland. Castle served Delaware in the US House of Representatives and was also Governor of Delaware.

The canal and adjacent land is owned by the US Army Corps of Engineers and managed by the Maryland Department of Natural Resources and the Delaware Department of Fish and Wildlife. The trail was constructed starting in 2012 and finished in late 2016. Only 1.8

miles of the trail is in Maryland; the rest is in Delaware. Cyclists who complete the entire Delaware portion can brag that they've ridden across the entire width of the First State (no need to mention that distance is only a bit over thirteen miles).

Trip Description

Begin your ride from the western end of the C&D Canal Trail, located at the foot of Lock Street in Chesapeake City, on the north side of the canal. As of this writing (2017), there is no dedicated parking area or any facilities located here, although planning for both is under consideration. The most convenient and legal local parking is one block east of the trailhead, under the bridge for Route 213, marked by a sign that this is overflow parking for Schaefer's Canal House restaurant.

The first mile of trail runs past the backyards of attractive houses in Chesapeake City, all homes on large lots that have taken advantage of the water views with the addition of decks and picture windows. There are benches for sitting and relaxing about every hundred yards, and the trail here in town is often used by the local citizenry for dog walking and strolling. Houses drop away in the second mile, and a low berm blocks any view from the trail of the adjacent Biddle Street. At mile 1.85, the trail enters Delaware.

For the next several miles, the character of the trail does not change. On one side is the water of the canal, separated from the trail by piles of boulders that break the wake of passing ships. Only a few hardy plants grow in the gaps between rocks. The opposite side of the trail is a hillside covered in small trees and shrubs that provide good habitat for sparrows, cardinals, and other birds that favor such brushy places. Indeed, the land bordering both shores is part of the C&D Canal Wildlife Area, more than 5,000 acres in size. Until the trail was constructed starting in 2012, it was the almost exclusive domain of hunters and fishermen. Now with increased usage by cyclists, joggers, hikers, and other participants in non-consumptive recreation, the word "Wildlife" has been replaced with "Conservation" in the name. Conflict between members of different user groups exists but has been minimal, and patrolling and enforcement of regulations is now more frequent.

One species of animal is fairly new to the C&D Canal Conservation

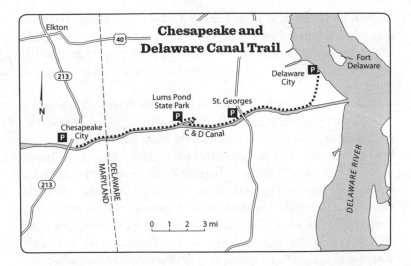

Area: the coyote. Delaware was the last state to be re-populated with coyotes, an event that probably occurred early in the twenty-first century. They are still uncommon; Delaware's first hunting season in 2014 yielded exactly one animal. Nevertheless, no species of predator adapts better to a human-dominated landscape than the coyote, and sightings will doubtless increase over time. Maryland was the second-to-last state to host coyotes. These canids are now found in every county and are seen with some frequency by alert citizens.

The C&D Canal spans the entire width of the Delmarva peninsula. As such, it was a barrier to the southward migration of coyotes. That barrier did not last long. The entire population of coyotes on the Eastern Shore likely are descended from animals that swam the 450-foot width of the canal, or crossed the ice on those rare days when the canal is frozen. The hardiness and dispersal ability of coyotes is amazing.

The middle portion of the C&D Canal Trail features several places where the trail leaves the canal and rises as much as 100 feet to the upland forest. The first is at mile 5.5, where the South Lums trailhead features parking and vault toilets. Shortly thereafter, the trail skirts an inlet off the canal, the Summit North Marina, where restrooms, water, and even a restaurant are located. These hills (remember, this is Delaware, so "hill" is a relative term) provide a welcome opportunity for the cyclist to use some new muscles and maybe even get a bit of an aerobic workout.

At mile 7.5, the trail passes under a railroad lift bridge, reminiscent of the familiar Tower Bridge in London. The center span of this lift bridge is high enough off the water to permit passage by the tallest container ships, but can be lowered to allow a train to cross it at grade.

The C&D Canal is far older than it appears today. As early as the 1700s local entrepreneurs realized that a canal across the Delmarva peninsula at its narrowest point would make the trip between the busy port of Baltimore and all points north on the Atlantic seaboard shorter by about 300 miles. Construction of a canal began in 1824, and the canal became operational just five years later. However, this canal was a pale imitation of the current waterway, being only 10 feet deep and 66 feet wide. This canal had four locks, to account for the different sea levels of Chesapeake Bay and Delaware Bay. The canal was bought by the US government in 1919, and for the next fifty years it was frequently widened and deepened in response to increasingly larger commercial ships. Today, at 450 feet wide and 35 feet deep, it is traversed by more than 25,000 boats and ships of all sizes. One of the rewards of cycling the C&D Canal Trail is viewing a towering oceangoing ship sailing past you just a few dozen yards away.

The easternmost half of the C&D Canal Trail seems less remote than the western portion. There are two trailhead access points, at St. George's and Biddle Point, and both are often busy with people there to fish, walk, or cycle. Within sight of the Delaware City water tower, the trail moves inland, passing over a wetland on a berm. At mile 14.4 is the refurbished graveyard of the African Union Church, which operated from 1835 to 1931. At least five veterans of the Civil War are buried here. During the Depression, the graveyard was abandoned, then reclaimed by vegetation, and finally lost from memory. In 1990, children playing in the area found an old engraved marker stone. Soon thereafter, the graveyard was restored, and it now holds an honored place in Delaware history.

A short distance east of the graveyard, the trail enters Delaware City proper, and for most of its final mile runs along the waterfront on brick pavers. It terminates at the Point, a small city park with views across Delaware Bay toward Pea Patch Island. On this island is Fort Delaware, which was used as a prisoner-of-war camp during the Civil War. In the warmer months, a ferry runs from Delaware City to the island, where there are tours, walking trails, and occasional

events. Bring a bike lock and chain so you can visit this interesting Delaware State Park.

Unless you have set up a car shuttle, it's another 15.6 miles back to Chesapeake City. Thirty-one miles is a long ride unless you cycle regularly, but with an asphalt surface and most of the trail running dead flat, it's easy to make those miles. Enjoy.

Directions

From Baltimore or Washington, DC, take I-95 north. Take exit 100A, Route 272, going south for 1.5 miles into the town of North East, Maryland. Turn left on Route 40, Pulaski Highway. Go 6.6 miles, then turn right on Route 213. Go 4.7 miles and turn left on Route 285. This road ends at the trailhead in Chesapeake City. The most convenient and legal local parking is one block east of the trailhead, under the bridge for Route 213, marked by a sign that this is overflow parking for Schaefer's Canal House restaurant.

Other Outdoor Recreational Opportunities Nearby

Elk Neck State Park and Fair Hill Natural Resources Management Area are both within a thirty-minute drive. In Delaware, Lums Pond State Park borders the midpoint of the C&D Canal Trail.

COYOTES

I watched as the coyote tempted the big dog with a clear canine invitation to play. The lab took off after the coyote at full speed, the coyote keeping just ahead at a pace that looked more like a trot than a run. They vanished into the forest.

Five minutes later, the big dog emerged from the trees into the meadow. Tongue out, moving slowly, tail down, the lab was clearly exhausted. Nipping at his heels was the coyote, seemingly as fresh as a daisy, just toying with the lab. Had the dog been smaller, or farther from home, he might never have returned to his family. As it was, he was lucky to get by with having learned a valuable lesson about coyotes. As had I.

Coyotes first arrived in Maryland in 1972, one of the last two states in the Union to host a breeding population of these adaptable canines. When European settlers arrived in North America, coyotes were animals of the Great Plains, occupying a range between the Mississippi River and the Rocky Mountains. During westward expansion, colonists killed off the top predators in the east, wolves and mountain lions. Coyotes moved to fill this predator vacuum, spreading eastward around the south end of the Appalachian Mountains and around the north side of the Great Lakes. It took more than 300 years, but these two spur groups finally reached Maryland within living memory. Coyotes were first documented in Washington, DC, in 2004, and in Baltimore City about the same time.

Along the way, those coyotes taking the Canadian route picked up some wolf genes. Both groups also picked up some genetic heritage from domestic dogs. Today, coyotes in the mid-Atlantic region are hybrids, averaging about 62 percent coyote, 27 percent wolf, and 11 percent dog. As a result of this blend, these coyotes are stockier and heavier than coyotes found in the Great Plains.

As newcomers to the Maryland scene, coyotes keep a lower profile here than elsewhere. For example, I have heard coyotes howling every night in a suburban neighborhood of Lake Tahoe, California, and can usually see them around dusk if I am observant. In contrast, I have never heard the coyotes who are sometimes seen near Patapsco Valley State Park. Coyotes howl as a way to maintain contact with others of their species. It's an unearthly sound, and a few coyotes can sound like at least a dozen.

Coyotes typically have a high rate of reproduction, often five to six pups annually. In areas where they are newly arrived on the scene, their population may increase by about 30 percent each year. Breeding occurs in winter and gestation lasts about two months, so the young are born as spring arrives. There are reports that coyotes prey on white-tailed deer fawns in late May, but adult deer are too large to become victims unless debilitated by disease or old age. Hence, coyotes cannot control the deer overpopulation problem even though they are the apex predator of our Maryland landscape.

An extraordinarily catholic diet is one major reason coyotes are so successful. While they probably prefer small mammals, they also eat berries, fruits, insects, birds, carrion, small farm animals, and domestic animals. Feral cats are rare where there are coyotes. When coyotes move in, red foxes either move out or are killed. But probably the most significant reason coyotes are so successful is their intelligence; they are able to persist, and even prosper, in a human-dominated landscape. Maryland citizens can expect to see coyotes more and more frequently in the years to come.

Three Notch Trail

Section: Northern Senior Center, Charlotte Hall, to John V. Baggett Memorial Park

County: St. Mary's

Distance: 9 miles one way, with a 4-mile round-trip spur

Type: Multi-use recreational trail

Surface: Asphalt

Difficulty: Easy. Flat

Hazards: Traffic at intersections

Highlights: Rural scenery

More information: St. Mary's County Department of Recreation and Parks, (301) 475-4200, ext. 71800

Street Address: 29655 Charlotte Hall Road, Charlotte Hall, Maryland 20622 (Northern Senior Center trailhead)

GPS Coordinates: 38.483115, 76.781367 (Northern Senior Center trailhead)

Running down the center of St. Mary's County in southern Maryland, the Three Notch Trail will eventually link the northern part of the county with the population centers in and near Lexington Park. Currently, 11 contiguous miles exist of what may one day become a 25- to 28-mile paved, off-road, multi-use recreational trail. This route was once a portion of the railbed of the old Washington, Brandywine, and Point Lookout Railroad, which was extended by the Navy in 1942 to service the newly built Patuxent River Naval Air Station. The Navy last used this rail line in 1954, occasional trains ran on it for another decade, and the abandoned right-of-way was purchased by St. Mary's County in 1970. The county began developing the Three Notch Trail in about 2005, after it had languished neglected and almost forgotten for years. Planning for the southern

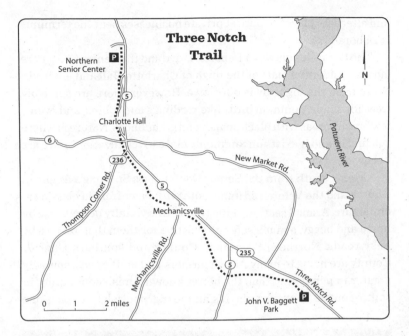

portion of the Three Notch Trail has just begun, and construction is probably at least a decade away.

The curious name of this trail comes from the adjacent Route 235, Three Notch Road. This old colonial road, in turn, took its name from a 1704 law that stated, "three notches of equal distance" shall be marked on trees to indicate a road leading to a ferry. The route runs along the spine of the county on the high ground separating the watersheds of the Patuxent and Potomac Rivers; lands to the east and west have some surprisingly steep ravines that would have required extensive bridging or grading to support a road.

Trip Description

The most convenient public access point near the northern end of the trail is at the Northern Senior Center in Charlotte Hall. There is plenty of free parking there as well as bathrooms in the building open during business hours. However, this location is two miles south of the northern terminus of the Three Notch Trail. Since this portion of the trail is parallel to Three Notch Road, Route 235, it is not hard to find alternate places to park at private businesses near the terminus at Deborah Drive.

The two miles between Deborah Drive and the Senior Center are mostly residential, part of the town of Charlotte Hall and environs. Noise from the highway is obtrusive. However, there are some big trees for shade, common birds like cardinals and robins, and even a few brushy areas with black snakes and groundhogs. Nature is where you find it, and it exists uncommonly close to "civilization" if we are but aware of it.

Cycling south from the Senior Center, pass St. Anne's Anglican Church and the Veteran's Home, both with beautiful old classic architecture. A small section of the trail in this vicinity permits use by horse and buggy, a much safer alternative for them than on nearby busy roads. Northern St. Mary's County and southern Charles County are home to many Amish farmers and craftsmen, reputedly greater in population than the better known Amish community in south-central Pennsylvania. It's an incongruous sight to pass one

of these buggies, straight out of the nineteenth century, while in a modern town like Charlotte Hall.

Once outside of town, you will pass by rural yards, horse pastures, and tidy farms. The trail shoulders have been planted in warm season grasses; the occasional red clover lends a touch of color to the scene. In a few places woodlots surround the trail, lending a pleasant cover on hot days, but a majority of the Three Notch trail lacks shade as it passes through such a pastoral landscape. There are numerous road crossings, but most are merely driveways to one or two houses. Still, use care at these crossings.

St. Mary's County was the site of Maryland's first colony, with settlers arriving in 1634. Many of these properties, therefore, have been farmed for more than 350 years. Tobacco was long a staple crop in southern Maryland, and there are still many old tobacco barns; several are visible from the trail. Tobacco wears out the soil, however, and most farms today grow corn, soybeans, and winter wheat in a two-year rotation.

After nine miles of pleasant cycling, the current southern terminus of the Three Notch Trail is reached at John V. Baggett Memorial Park. Shade, picnic tables, modern restrooms, drinking water, athletic fields, and plenty of parking can be found here. Unless you have spotted a second car here to help with a shuttle, this is your halfway point. Since the trail is dead flat and arrow straight, the return trip is no more strenuous than the ride was to this point. Enjoy a pleasant cycle back.

Directions

From the Washington, DC, Beltway (I-495), take exit 7 for Route 5, Branch Avenue, south. Go 26 miles. Turn right on Charlotte Hall Road and go 1.5 miles; Northern Senior Center is on the right. From the Baltimore Beltway (I-695), take either I-95 or I-295 south to the DC Beltway, I-495, and follow the above directions.

Other Outdoor Recreational Opportunities Nearby

Nothing close; the Indian Head Trail is a thirty-minute drive to the northwest of Charlotte Hall.

MONARCH BUTTERFLIES

Insects as a group are often looked upon with distaste; many have unusual or bizarre bodies, and others are associated with disease, pestilence, or filth. The exception to this generalization is the lepidopteran order, which includes butterflies and moths. Among the butterflies, perhaps none is more familiar than the beautiful orange and black monarch. A numerous and widespread species, monarchs nevertheless pose a dilemma for modern science. Researchers still do not understand how such neurologically simple organisms can migrate thousands of miles each fall to wintering sites none of them has ever before seen.

Monarch butterfly eggs are laid exclusively on milkweed plants. The pale green eggs hatch, and the boldly striped yellow, black, and white caterpillars feed on the juices of their host plant. They molt four times and then transform into a quiescent pupal stage. Over a period of several days, the body structure is completely rearranged, and eventually a butterfly emerges. Two or three generations occur each summer, so that the butterflies that migrate south in August are not the same ones that arrived in late spring.

In late summer, the last generation of the year begins to drift slowly southward. Butterflies cluster at the south ends of peninsulas like Cape May, Cape Charles, and Point Lookout, awaiting favorable winds that will aid them in their flight over open water. By November, monarchs from the East Coast arrive in the mountains of south central Mexico to spend the winter at a single roost site that is only a few acres in size.

The butterflies roost in oyamel fir trees in this one location where the temperature and humidity are just right. They cover entire trees in a spectacular display but are torpid and may die if disturbed in any way. In fact, only about 1 percent survive the winter to fly north in the spring. Surprisingly, these winter roost sites were discovered by scientists only in the mid-1970s. Since then, efforts to protect the sensitive butterflies and their roost sites have been underway. However, even if this area is well protected, changes in climate due to global warming threaten the persistence of this unique roost site.

The number of monarchs arriving in Mexico has been declining in recent years. On average, about 300 million butterflies overwinter there, but in 2015 just 42 million arrived. In large measure, this worrisome decline is due to loss of the monarch's obligate plant partner, milkweed. Milkweed declined 21 percent between 1995 and 2013, in large measure due to agricultural practices in the central United States. With corn prices up, farmers plowed right up to the property line in order to maximize yield, whereas in the past these edges often lay fallow, growing weeds that included milkweed. In addition, as of 2013, about 90 percent of the corn grown in the United States is herbicide resistant; when farmers spray herbicide to control weeds in the cornfield, herbicide drift may kill milkweed at the field edges.

Taken together, these threats to one of our most beautiful and fascinating animals is disturbing. In the next few decades, monarch butterflies may become far less common in the fields and gardens of America. Planting common milkweed in a sunny location on your property may help conserve monarchs, and moreover will provide you with an intimate view of the inner workings of our natural world.

Indian Head Trail

Section: Indian Head to White Plains
County: Charles
Distance: 13 miles one way
Type: Multi-use recreational trail
Surface: Asphalt
Difficulty: Easy. Flat
Hazards: Road crossings
Highlights: Extensive forests, wetlands
More information: Charles County Department of Recreation, Parks, and Tourism, (301) 932-3470
Street Address: Near 14 Mattingly Avenue, Indian Head, Maryland 20640 (Indian Head trailhead); 10410 Theodore Green Boulevard, White Plains, Maryland 20695 (White Plains trailhead)
GPS Coordinates: 38.597066, 77.168259 (Indian Head trailhead); 38.592112, 76.947112 (White Plains trailhead)

The watershed of Mattawoman Creek, in southern Maryland, is considered one of the most pristine in the state. Its water quality is excellent, development is still minimal, and its biological diversity remains mostly intact relative to pre-colonial times. A glance at a map of Maryland, however, shows that Mattawoman Creek is on the edge of the metastatic proliferation of houses and roads spreading ever outward from Washington, DC. In the face of such development pressure, can the area maintain its rural character and its attendant quality of life? The future is uncertain.

First opened in 2009, the Indian Head Trail runs along the abandoned railbed of the long defunct Indian Head and White Plains Railroad. Built in 1919 to service the Indian Head Naval Proving Ground, ᵗʰe railroad connected that base with the Pennsylvania Central

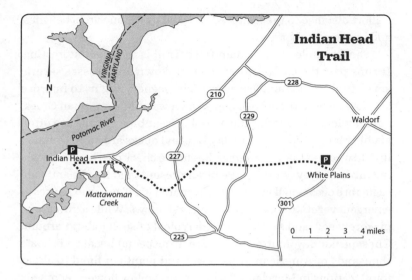

Railroad near Waldorf, Maryland. The rail line opened too late to be of use for World War I, but by the start of World War II, when the proving ground was one of only two facilities in the United States that could manufacture high explosives, the rail line was busy. By the 1950s, the base began to be serviced primarily by trucks, the railway was used less and less, and it was eventually abandoned. The federal government conveyed the right-of-way to Charles County in 2006. The naval base at Indian Head remains active.

Trip Description

This ride is described from west to east, beginning at Indian Head, because this trailhead is probably the most convenient for cyclists arriving from the Washington, DC, metro area. Baltimore-area cyclists may find the White Plains trailhead, just off Route 301, to be slightly closer for them, but the driving difference is shorter only by about five miles.

There is no public parking adjacent to the trail's origin in the town of Indian Head, but there is plenty within a few hundred yards. Charlie Wright Park, on the right side of Route 210 just before the entrance to the naval base, is the most convenient. It's just behind the post office. Restrooms and drinking water are available here. From the Park, cross Route 210 and ride down Mattingly Avenue for a short distance to the trailhead, marked by a stone arch, benches, and information boards.

The first mile of the Indian Head Trail is the least interesting. It runs past the backyards of the little town and crosses several small public roads and driveways. The scenery begins to improve at mile 2, where there are expansive views of Mattawoman Creek, here a wide tidal freshwater marsh. Great blue herons are often visible year-round, and Canada geese and ducks are more common in cold weather than in summer. Be sure to check overhead for soaring birds of prey; vultures are often present, and hawks and bald eagles are occasional visitors. In the marsh itself, green expanses of emergent vegetation carpet the muddy shallows. While arrow arum, pickerelweed, and spatterdock are typical of such habitat around Chesapeake Bay, Mattawoman Creek is special because it hosts thousands of American lotus, a wetland plant confined to about four locations in Maryland. Their creamy yellow flowers, about six inches in diameter and sitting like cups atop green leafy saucers, are exceptionally pretty.

On the opposite side of the trail, across from the Mattawoman Creek viewpoint, is a steep hillside where the native trees and shrubs have been entirely carpeted by kudzu. This invasive vine, originally from Asia, grows quickly and can kill the trees it drapes. However, kudzu is easily controlled by grazing, and so is common only on steep slopes along railroads and highways, like at this location. Furthermore, kudzu reaches it northernmost range in Maryland; to the north, cold winters prevent its growth. Still, there is something almost sinister about how it covers trees and power lines with a fatal green net.

The remaining ten miles of the Indian Head Trail are similar in character and make for an exceedingly pleasant ride. The view is almost always of maturing forest; only a few houses are visible from the trail in this still rural area. Long stretches are arrow-straight. There are wide shoulders that are kept mowed; the entire trail corridor, path and shoulders, is close to 100 feet in width. Note how the first line of trees has grown over the trail in search of sunlight; many have arching branches more than 45 degrees from the vertical, forming a green, open-roofed tunnel. However, because of the distance of the trees from the bike path, the trail itself is not shaded at midday, and in summer can be quite hot.

Probably the most interesting part of the Indian Head Trail is the pond and wetland at the exact halfway point. Created by the berms of the railbed and Bumpy Oak Road, the wetland is dotted with long-dead trees that stand like skeletons about the landscape. Woodpeckers drill for insects in the rotting wood and excavate cavities for nesting in those standing snags that are still solid. While familiar forest woodpeckers like the downy, red-bellied, and pileated are all common here, red-headed woodpeckers can also be sighted (with luck). These are unmistakable woodpeckers, with their entire head a cherry red in color and a large and conspicuous white rump patch amid otherwise black feathers. Red-heads have a cosmopolitan diet, including nuts, seeds, acorns, fruits, mice, insects, and even bird eggs. They have been known to sequester live grasshoppers into crevices in tree bark for their later dining pleasure. Since red-headed woodpeckers are uncommon throughout most of Maryland, count yourself lucky if you see a member of this local population.

In the open water of the pond is a large beaver lodge, easily viewed from the trail. Beavers are mostly nocturnal, so your best chance of seeing one is near dusk, as it hauls a freshly chopped tree limb across the trail to its home. A family of beavers can easily take down a thousand small trees in a year, in consonance with the phrase, "busy as a beaver." In most areas where beaver are present, trees a foot or more in diameter, gnawed partway or all the way around the circumference of the tree, can be found. Because the teeth of beaver grow continuously, they need to gnaw wood, like these large trees, to keep their incisors in good condition.

In the final mile, approaching the town of White Plains, a few houses and apartment buildings are visible through a scrim of trees, and foot traffic on the trail picks up. Two ponds host Canada geese and ducks in autumn and a noisy crowd of amphibians in spring. The White Plains trailhead, on Theodore Green Boulevard just off Route 301, has ample parking, drinking water, and portable restrooms.

Directions

From the Washington, DC, Beltway (I-495), take exit 3, Route 210, south toward Indian Head, for twenty miles. Leave your car near Charlie Wright Park, on the right just before the entrance to the naval base, behind the post office. Baltimore cyclists should take either I-95 or I-295 to the DC Beltway (I-495), and then follow the above directions.

Alternatively, the White Plains trailhead may be reached from Baltimore by taking I-97 south from the Baltimore Beltway (I-695). Take exit 7 for Route 3, which eventually becomes Route 301. In the town of White Plains, just south of Waldorf, turn right on Theodore Green Boulevard and go a quarter mile to the trailhead.

Other Outdoor Recreational Opportunities Nearby

There is excellent canoeing and kayaking on Mattawoman Creek, located at the foot of Mattingly Avenue about a quarter mile from the Indian Head trailhead.

THE CHESAPEAKE BAY BOLIDE EVENT

It's a beautiful morning near present-day Richmond, Virginia, 35.5 million years ago. The air is warm and humid, and the vegetation is tropical, even though the short days and long nights say "winter." The ocean laps gently at the shore; the planet's greenhouse-like environment means there are no polar icecaps, and so the sea covers what is now the coastal plain of Maryland and Virginia. Exotic mammals, ancestors of the types we know today, graze peacefully.

Suddenly, there is a blinding flash of light; a bolide (comet or asteroid) streaks across the sky and impacts the ocean offshore. The bolide torpedoes through the shallow waters and buries itself in the ocean floor to a depth of almost five miles. Instantly, millions of tons of water, sediments, and fractured rock are ejected into the air, creating a cloud that does not dissipate for days or weeks. A tsunami is generated; a wall of water 1,500 feet high surges across the landscape, stopped only when it reaches the rampart of the Blue Ridge Mountains. The devastation is immense. The Chesapeake Bay bolide creates the largest impact crater in what is now the United States, and the sixth largest known on the planet. The crater is 25 miles in diameter, and as the adjacent sediments slide into the hole, it expands to more than 50 miles wide.

In the last half century, scientists have begun to understand how significant meteor impacts can be. The mass extinction of 65 million years ago, when dinosaurs suddenly disappear from the fossil record, is now thought to be due to an asteroid impact event. Another major extinction occurred 33.9 million years ago

(continued)

and may have been due to a combination of climate change, the Chesapeake Bay bolide, and the similar Popigai bolide impact in Siberia about this time. For life on Earth, there is nothing so catastrophic as a large meteor colliding with our planet.

Even though the Chesapeake Bay bolide event occurred tens of millions of years ago, its effects can still be seen. The crater occupies what is now the mouth of Chesapeake Bay, although buried far underneath more recent sediment deposits. A glance at a map shows that all the major rivers of the region flow toward this location: the Susquehanna, Potomac, Rappahannock, James, and York. The latter two rivers take a curious jog to the northeast; they do so as they encounter the location of the crater's outer wall.

Just after the impact, the ejecta settled to earth, some of it landing in the crater and creating a jumbled mass of rubble. Surrounding sediments also slumped into the crater, making the geology even more disorganized. Fault lines formed and remain. There have been four recorded earthquakes here, the most recent in 1995. The rock and sediments of the crater continue to settle and are thought to contribute to the ground subsidence that still occurs on the Eastern Shore and tidewater Virginia.

Another effect of the impact crater was that the area filled with a huge reservoir of hypersaline water. This aquifer was later covered by sediments, and freshwater aquifers lie above it. Nevertheless, places like Portsmouth, Virginia, are chronically short of drinking water because wells often come up contaminated with salt. For example, during the Civil War, soldiers at Fort Monroe dug a well but abandoned the task when, at more than 900 feet of depth, only saline water was to be found. There is concern even today that deep-well drilling could penetrate the hypersaline layer and lead to contamination of the freshwater aquifers.

A study of bolide impacts like this one in the Chesapeake is both fascinating and disturbing. Not only are the immediate effects devastating on a regional or even global level, but those effects echo down the millennia. The question that arises is: when will the next large bolide impact Earth, and what effect will it have on humans and the other life forms that share the planet with us?

Washington, Baltimore, and Annapolis (WB&A) Trail

Section: Section 1: Odenton to the Patuxent River
Section 2: Patuxent River to MD Route 450, Lanham
County: Section 1: Anne Arundel
Section 2: Prince George's
Distance: Section 1: 5.9 miles one way
Section 2: 7.2 miles one way
Type: Multi-use recreational trail
Surface: Asphalt
Difficulty: Section 1: Easy. Slightly rolling terrain with one long hill
Section 2: Easy. Slightly rolling terrain
Hazards: Road crossings
Highlights: River floodplain forest, Coastal Plain nature preserve
More information: Section 1: Anne Arundel County Department of
Recreation and Parks, (410) 222-6141
Section 2: Prince George's County Department of Parks and Recreation,
(301) 699-2255
Street Address: Section 1: Near 1350 Odenton Road, Odenton,
Maryland 21113
Section 2: Near 8660 Race Track Road, Bowie, Maryland 20715
GPS Coordinates: Section 1: 39.083754, 76.700089 (Odenton origin of trail)
Section 2: 39.009622, 76.746378 (Race Track Road parking area)

O f all the bike trails in Maryland, perhaps the most schizo-phrenic is the Washington, Baltimore, and Annapolis Trail. Commonly referred to merely as the WB&A Trail, it consists of two sections divided by the Patuxent River. It has always been the goal of trail planners to link these two segments with a bridge, but somehow it has never quite been accomplished. Between hostile landowners, environmental considerations, and bureaucratic squabbling, almost two decades has elapsed without a bridge. A welcome sense of urgency and an increased spirit of cooperation eventually emerged between the two counties, in partnership with the State of Maryland, and in 2016 new asphalt was laid, bringing each end of the trail to within 100 yards of the river. As of this writing, there are definite plans for the bridge, and a funding mechanism is in place. Before you ride this trail, check with one of the two managing agencies for updates on trail construction.

Despite the name Washington, Baltimore, and Annapolis Trail, the WB&A does not come close to any of these three cities. Rather, the trail is built on the right-of-way of the long-abandoned Washington, Baltimore, and Annapolis Electric Railway, a commuter line with an interesting social history. In 1917, as the United States entered World War I, the politically well-connected president of the WB&A convinced the federal government to establish a military base that is now Fort Meade. By war's end, up to 84 special trains a day were supplying the new base, and the WB&A was briefly profitable. The railway was also instrumental in the establishment of Bowie Race Track, providing a means to bring spectators to horse racing events, a sport far more popular a century ago than it is today. Finally, the management persuaded legislators in Annapolis to exempt the WB&A from state taxes (although with the onset of the Depression this valuable perk was rescinded). With the rise of auto and truck transportation, the line went bankrupt in 1935, and much of the right-of-way lay abandoned until 2000.

The Anne Arundel County portion of the WB&A Trail has a different feel to it relative to the Prince George's County segment. Much of the trail in Anne Arundel is bordered by new and upscale housing developments, with tidy landscaping and well-maintained houses. The planned community of Piney Orchard even has a large nature preserve that borders the trail, with public footpaths that invite exploration. In contrast, the Prince George's section is a bit older, the asphalt bumpier, and in several places it shares that paving with private driveways and their attendant cars. Even so, the entire length of trail is pleasant and a valuable addition to the pantheon of safe, off-road cycling and walking paths that are such a wonderful Maryland recreational amenity.

Trip Description

Section 1: Odenton to the Patuxent River

The WB&A Trail begins without fanfare in Odenton, Maryland, at the intersection of Odenton Road and Piney Orchard Parkway. There is a tiny, neatly kept park here called Babington Green; food, drink, and restrooms are available in nearby businesses. Initially a sidewalk adjacent to busy Piney Orchard Parkway, the trail soon tops the hill and begins a long, shallow descent. A façade of trees hides most views of the surrounding neighborhoods, but a power line shares the right-of-way. At mile 1.2, cross busy Waugh Chapel Road, and then Strawberry Lakes Way at mile 2.4.

Just beyond this point, consider chaining your bike to the available rack and walk the trail into the 45-acre Piney Orchard Nature Preserve. There are several miles of trail through maturing forest, past dense wetlands, and around two ponds filled with water lilies. The entire area was once a sand and gravel mine; the abandoned pits have filled with water that attract birds like great blue herons, green herons, and a variety of ducks.

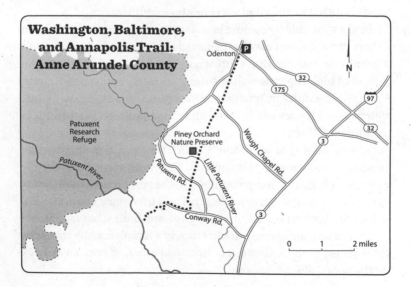

Back on the WB&A Trail, cross the Little Patuxent River; the floodplain forest surrounding it is home to a variety of songbirds, some of whom are year-round residents and some of whom are here only for a few months in late spring and early summer. Just beyond Patuxent Road, mile 3.3, a large abandoned gravel pit hosts a variety of wildlife, including cricket frogs, wood ducks, painted turtles, and mud turtles. Just beyond this pond the trail passes under a major power line, where summer grasses and flowers like crown vetch, yarrow, and tickseed sunflower bloom. Ahead is the Two Rivers community, an extensive new housing development. In an agreement with the county and state, the developer extended the WB&A Trail for 1.4 miles through here in 2016, including the series of switchbacks that lead down to the floodplain of the Patuxent River. These switchbacks, actually wide sweeping turns, descend for at least 100 feet of elevation change; control your speed on this long downhill. As of this writing, the bridge across the Patuxent has not yet been built, so this portion of the WB&A Trail ends abruptly near the river.

Section 2: Patuxent River to MD Route 450, Lanham
The WB&A Trail continues on the Prince George's County side of the Patuxent River. Since as of this writing there is no bridge across the river, a convenient access point to this portion of the trail is a designated parking lot off Race Track Road in Bowie. There are portable toilets here but no drinking water or other facilities.

Begin your ride by cycling in a southeasterly direction. Within a short distance, you may be dismayed by the sound of gunfire, but it is only the Berwyn Gun Club, whose property abuts the trail. An eight-foot high concrete wall ensures your safety from stray rounds. A bit farther south, the trail passes a beautiful horse farm, with neat whitewashed fences and graceful elms shading green pastures. It is truly a pastoral scene.

The remaining miles of the WB&A Trail are a mix of suburban backyards and pockets of woodland. The trail shares the right-of-way with a high-tension power line, so the vegetation is kept short by episodic mowing. Berry bushes thrive in this sunny environment, so look for dewberries, black raspberries, and their relatives at midsummer, a welcome snack on a hot day. In a few places, the trail provides access to the driveways of isolated homes, so keep an eye out for the occasional automobile.

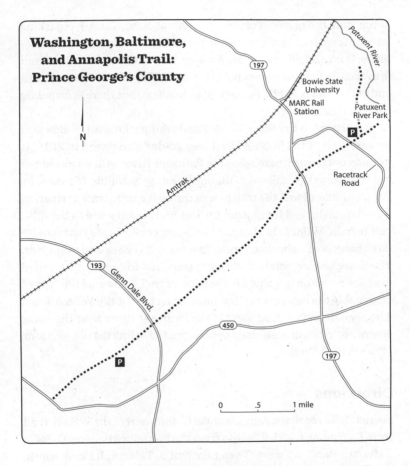

Washington, Baltimore, and Annapolis Trail: Prince George's County

Prince George's County residents may wish to stop at the Glenn Dale Community Center and Splash Park at about mile 4 (summers only). The rest of us non-resident cyclists can only look on with envy at the cooling frivolities. Just past this park is the Department of Agriculture property where the famous Glenn Dale azaleas were bred; hundreds of varieties may be seen at the National Arboretum in Washington, DC. A bit farther still is the 216-acre property of the former Glenn Dale Hospital, a tuberculosis sanatorium that operated from 1934 to 1981. Almost two dozen buildings still stand, all in disrepair and contaminated with asbestos and lead paint.

As the WB&A Trail nears its southern terminus, it passes a small pond. A few standing dead trees are home to woodpeckers and tree swallows, while red-winged blackbirds and the occasional great blue heron stalk the marsh. Turtles and frogs abound. There is a parking lot here for a dozen cars, as well as portable toilets, but no other amenities. It is reached by Electric Avenue, just off Glenn Dale Road, and is the southernmost access point for the WB&A Trail. The technical end of the trail is at MD Route 450 in Lanham, but there is no public parking there.

Returning to the Race Track Road trail parking lot in Bowie, a new section of the WB&A Trail was graded and paved in 2016. It extends northward, parallel to the Patuxent River, still on an old rail bed that keeps the trail out of the surrounding wetlands. Managed by Patuxent River Park, the trail passes through a large tract of riparian forest, undisturbed for at least the last half century due to the difficult terrain. Wildlife is abundant here, especially birds that require large parcels of unbroken forest, like wood thrushes and ovenbirds. There are beaver ponds, and river otters, red fox, and white-tailed deer are common but shy. This section of trail, known as the "spur," is arguably the most scenic and interesting part of the WB&A Trail. The asphalt ends within view of the Patuxent River near the point where a bridge will eventually be constructed to link the two sections of the WB&A Trail.

Directions

Section 1: To reach the Anne Arundel County part of the WB&A Trail from Baltimore, take I-97 south from the Baltimore Beltway (I-695). Exit onto Route 32 west. Then take exit 5, Telegraph Road, south. Go about one mile to the intersection with Odenton Road (near this point Telegraph Road becomes Piney Orchard Parkway). From Washington, DC, take I-95 north from the Beltway (I-495). Exit onto Route 32 east. Then take exit 5, Telegraph Road, south. Go about one mile to the intersection with Odenton Road (near this point Telegraph Road becomes Piney Orchard Parkway).

Section 2: To reach the Prince George's County part of the WB&A Trail, take the Baltimore-Washington Parkway (I-295), from either Washington or Baltimore. Exit onto Route 197 east. Just past Bowie State University, turn left on Race Track Road. Go about one mile to the trail parking area on the left. If you reach the site of the old Bowie racetrack, you have gone too far.

Other Outdoor Recreational Opportunities Nearby

Greenbelt Park, with several hiking trails, is located a short drive to the east, while Patuxent National Wildlife Refuge is several miles to the north.

CANOPY CLOSURE

The most significant ecological event of the natural year in Maryland is canopy closure. After almost six months without leaves, deciduous trees leaf out in the spring and begin a season of photosynthesis. That process, taking carbon dioxide from the air and using sunlight to transform it into usable biological chemicals, is the basis of the food chain that permits animal life on our planet. Canopy closure occurs when the newly formed leaves of trees reach a density such that they shade the forest floor.

Some native Maryland trees, like pines and hollies, remain green year-round. But the vast majority of our trees go quiescent in the colder months, dropping their burden of leaves so as to avoid damage by snow and ice. In October, chlorophyll and other pigments are resorbed from the leaves and stored in the roots and other tissues of the tree. Only the inert cellulose skeleton of the leaf falls to earth. In spring, as temperatures warm and day length increases, building-block chemicals like sugars move up into the branches, where their energy is used to catalyze the growth of new leaves.

Warming temperatures in spring also rouse insects from their winter sleep, and they are hungry. Tender young leaves are a favorite food for many kinds of insects, and they graze voraciously. Once fully expanded, leaves begin to manufacture chemicals that discourage insects from eating them, and so the leaves become less palatable. But in April and May, new green leaves are a veritable salad bar for phytophagous insects.

Canopy closure is a significant event for birds as well. Insects, particularly caterpillars, are the favored diet of many migratory bird species, especially warblers. These tiny birds arrive in

(continued)

Maryland between mid-April and mid-May, the exact season when trees are beginning to leaf out, dining on the bugs that are now so plentiful. Without this windfall of insect food, warblers and other insectivorous songbirds could not complete their migration to points north for their nesting season. Meanwhile, our local year-round resident birds, as well as some now-resident migrants, begin building nests, laying eggs, and raising young here in Maryland. And it's not just the plethora of insect food that is important. Canopy closure permits nests to be at least partially hidden, reducing predation on eggs and nestlings.

Down on the forest floor, canopy closure and its concomitant reduction in sunlight reaching ground level signals the end of the blooming season for springtime ephemeral wildflowers like spring beauties, trout lilies, Dutchman's breeches, windflowers, and even the non-native invasive lesser celandine. In the cool early months of spring, these low-growing floral gems have used the abundant sunlight to grow, flower, and set seed. Within a few weeks of canopy closure, all will have died back and will spend the next ten months underground as bulbs, corms, and rhizomes. Although a new suite of forest wildflowers emerges after canopy closure, they are fewer in diversity, number, and acreage covered.

So canopy closure is a supremely important ecological event in the cycle of seasons. But it is also one of the most aesthetically pleasing occasions each year. Day by day, we humans watch trees become greener and greener; the season literally changes daily before our very eyes. That singular lime green color of newly formed buds has no other match in the natural world. After months of a drab winter landscape, we can rejoice in the annual renewal of life, a sign of hope and faith for a better world in the months to come.

Baltimore and Annapolis Trail

Section: Glen Burnie to Boulter's Way, near Annapolis
County: Anne Arundel
Distance: 13.3 miles one way; 10.5 miles one way as described
Type: Multi-use recreational trail
Surface: Asphalt
Difficulty: Easy. Flat
Hazards: Road crossings
Highlights: Suburban backyards, with some natural forests
More Information: Anne Arundel County Department of Recreation and
   Parks, (410) 222-6244
Street Address: 51 West Earleigh Heights Road, Severna Park, Maryland
   21146 (administrative headquarters); 7900 Ritchie Highway, Glen Burnie,
   Maryland 21061 (Marley Station Mall)
GPS Coordinates: 39.097027, 76.569739 (Earleigh Heights headquarters);
   39.137346, 76.607657 (Marley Station Mall); 39.010088, 76.488859
   (Boulter's Way trail parking area)

There are few places in Maryland more thoroughly suburban than the strip development lining both sides of Ritchie Highway (Route 2) in Anne Arundel County between Glen Burnie and Annapolis. Until 1989, this was the only good road between Baltimore and the Bay Bridge, and weekends found interminable lines of cars creeping along in stop-and-go fashion between innumerable red lights. Businesses sprang up adjacent to the highway in an effort to strip-mine frustrated tourists from the lines of traffic. Yet running along the rear of the shopping centers, parallel to Route 2, is another

55

world. The Baltimore and Annapolis (B&A) Trail, a paved thread of asphalt laid on the old railroad grade, runs for over thirteen miles past pocket wetlands and under large trees. Considering that more than 140,000 people live within a mile of the B&A Trail, it maintains a surprisingly sylvan nature.

That's not to say that the B&A Trail will give you the same sort of experience as, say, the more rural Northern Central Railroad Trail; it won't. On weekends, that same accessibility and popularity make the B&A excessively crowded. There are many road crossings where bikes must be dismounted and walked. In places, housing developments line the trail. But an early morning ride can still reveal a woodpecker drumming on an old tree or a garter snake slithering across the pavement.

The B&A Trail is currently 13.3 miles long, running arrow straight and dead flat for most of its length. For this reason, it is suitable for cyclists of all ages and makes a fine practice road for young riders on training wheels. People using wheelchairs and strollers will also be able to navigate the trail easily. Be sure to keep an eye on younger riders at the many road crossings.

It is possible to extend your ride significantly by continuing beyond the north end of the B&A Trail. A well-marked and paved connector trail leads to the Baltimore-Washington International Airport (BWI) Trail. This 10.1-mile loop is scenic and features an excellent location for viewing arriving and departing aircraft at close range. It is described elsewhere in this book.

Trip Description

The B&A Trail is managed and patrolled by the Anne Arundel County Department of Recreation and Parks. The department provides two parking lots for trail patrons, one at the south end off Boulter's Way and the other in the middle at Earleigh Heights Road. In addition, there are many private shopping center lots on the east side of Route 2 that could be used. But by far the most common starting point is Marley Station Mall, at mile 2.8, near the junction of Route 100 and Route 2. This access point provides unlimited parking and is a well-known landmark. Bathrooms are available in the mall, as is the usual assortment of fast food restaurants. Bike racks are found at trail's edge.

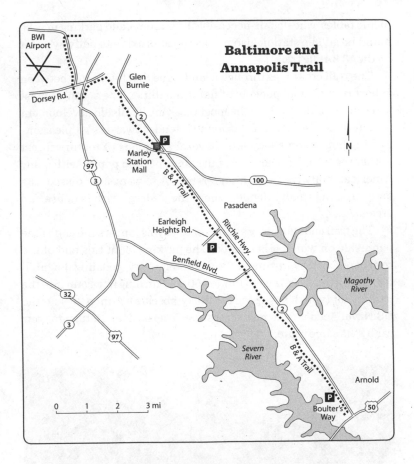

From Marley Station, the trail stretches 2.8 miles to the north, traversing the backyards of suburban Glen Burnie. This portion of the trail is a bit less enjoyable because of the developed nature of the neighborhood, and most trail users choose to pedal southward.

As the trail leaves the rear of Marley Station Mall and crosses over Route 100, it passes through dry, sandy woods. The twisted and irregular branches of Virginia pine dominate the overstory, and on hot days the pungent odor of pine wafts over the trail. Also present are sweet gum trees, most noticeable in autumn when their spiked fruit balls litter the trail like vegetable caltrops. Long, tawny grasses sweep back and forth in the breeze.

The Earleigh Heights ranger station, a renovated 1890s-era grocery store, is located at mile 6.8. Information, a few exhibits, water, picnic tables, wheelchair-accessible bathrooms, and parking may be found here. The station also marks the approximate halfway point on the 13.3-mile trail.

The trail continues through a landscape that alternates between suburbia and small pockets of natural habitat. The southernmost three miles of the trail are the most pleasant. Trailside development is more sparse, and where it is found it tends toward large, pleasant-looking houses on shady lots. Several stretches of mature forest border the trail, featuring fine, tall stands of tulip poplar with many American holly trees as an understory A few streams dissect the land, creating small hillsides where the undergrowth is dense and green.

The trail ends abruptly at Boulter's Way, as it nears the end of the peninsula on which it is located. The parking lot at this end of the trail is reached by turning left on Boulter's Way, pedaling downhill for about a third of a mile to Route 450, and turning left again into the parking lot (which has space for thirty-six cars). Annapolis and the US Naval Academy lie just across the Severn River. Return to your car by the same route.

Directions

To reach Marley Station Mall from Baltimore, take the Route 2 south exit from the Baltimore Beltway (I-695). The mall is about four miles south, on the right.

From Washington, it may be more convenient to park near the southern terminus of the trail. From the Capital Beltway (I-495), take Route 50 east. Near Annapolis, take exit 27 south. Once on Route 450, go a few hundred feet to the B&A Trail parking lot on the right.

Other Outdoor Recreational Opportunities Nearby

The north end of the B&A Trail connects with the BWI Trail, presenting a fine opportunity for more cycling.

FIREFLIES

Evening settles slowly over the lawns and forest edges of Maryland in June; dew gathers on the grass in the thick, humid air. It's a sweet, magical time, when adults gather to chat while children romp for the last time before bed. In the gloaming, lights appear, blinking on and off, silent and mysterious as the dark watches of night. What child has not gazed and wondered at the lightning bug, perhaps our most familiar and engaging insect?

Lightning bugs are beetles, insects with leathery, veinless wings that meet in a straight line down the back. These fireflies are the only group of insects that can make controlled flashes of light; they do so to attract and find mates. In Maryland, there are at least six species of firefly within the genus *Photinus*, the most common group; *Photinus pyralis* is the most numerous species seen flashing over suburban lawns.

Fireflies overwinter as larvae, buried in the soil, and emerge in spring to feed, usually in wet or swampy areas. The larvae are predatory, feeding on snails and small insects, but little is known

(continued)

about this portion of the lightning bug life cycle. By late May, the larvae form pupae, emerging as the familiar fireflies just over two weeks later. By mid- to late June, fireflies are on the wing at dusk.

Actually, only male lightning bugs fly. Females, which in some species lack wings altogether, remain near the ground, climbing grass blades or other low vegetation. When ready to mate, a female responds to the light signals from a flying male with a brief flash of her own, orienting her abdominal lamp toward the male. The responding male flies closer and repeats his signal, and the process is reiterated until the two beetles find each other. After mating, the female lays eggs in the soil; these develop into the larval stage, completing the life cycle.

The several species of firefly that live in our area avoid one another by means of behavioral adaptations. Each species has its own characteristic flash duration and response time, to which other species will not respond. Firefly species also segregate by habitat and by time of night for flashing. Our common local firefly, *Photinus pyralis*, begins flashing as early as 20 minutes before sunset and remains active for about 45 minutes.

The flight path of a male *Pyralis* firefly is a J-shaped hop. The firefly sinks a little, flashes on as he approaches the bottom of the signature, begins to rise, and then flashes off early in the rise phase. The remainder of the upstroke of the J is completed in darkness. He then flies on to another prospective flash location, sinking as he does so, and repeats the signature. The whole flash pattern lasts for about 6 seconds at 70° Fahrenheit, and the flash itself lasts about half a second. Females respond about 2.5 seconds later, with a flash duration of half a second.

By imitating the "call" of a female firefly with a covered flashlight, you can attract males. Place a penlight or other small flashlight over your hand so that just a dim glow emerges through the tissue. When a male flashes nearby, signal as if you are a female. With some practice, you should be able to get male fireflies to land on your hand within a few flash sequences.

Patuxent Research Refuge: North Tract

Section: Research Refuge Contact Station to terminus and return
County: Anne Arundel
Distance: 16.0 miles as described; out-and-back ride
Type: Very lightly traveled refuge road
Surface: Asphalt, but cracked and broken in places
Difficulty: Easy to moderate. Rolling, but no steep or long hills
Hazards: Uneven pavement
Highlights: Second-growth forest, floodplain forest, land recovering
from abuse
More Information: Patuxent Research Refuge, https://fws.gov/refuge
/patuxent, (301) 497-5770
Street Address: 230 Bald Eagle Drive, Laurel, Maryland 20724
GPS Coordinates: 39.077749, 76.771845 (Bald Eagle Drive Contact Station)

The Baltimore-Washington corridor has been one of the fastest-growing areas in the United States for at least half a century. Each year, development takes woods, fallow lands, once-productive farms, and privately owned open space, converting them into housing tracts, strip malls, and superhighways. The density of people increases each year, and commuters become ever more frustrated with jammed roads and gridlock. The suburbs of Washington now overlap with the suburbs of Baltimore, and no end to the process seems to be in sight. Yet in the exact middle of this crowded metropolis lies the largest contiguous tract of forest in central Maryland, held in the public domain and protected from development. Largely unknown to most citizens, portions of the Patuxent National Wildlife Refuge opened for public visitation in 1991.

Known as the Patuxent Research Refuge, this 7,600-acre tract once was a part of Fort Meade when it was a field training center for the army. Much of the land was kept in its natural state for years, although it was heavily used by vehicles (including tanks) and soldiers on foot. As the Department of Defense budget was reduced in the late 1980s and early 1990s, this portion of Fort Meade was deemed superfluous. After much debate, the adjacent Patuxent Wildlife Research Center was named the supervisory agency. The land is to be managed for the conservation, research, and educational activities of the center, but also to maintain biological diversity for the protection of native and migratory species. Finally, the new property is to be open to the public for compatible recreational uses.

Eight miles of paved roads traverse the North Tract and make a fine bike trail. Although this road is open to cars, it is sparsely used, mostly by hunters and fishermen, and the speed limit is 25 mph. The route is not flat, but hills are mostly minor. Years of use and abuse have rutted this road, and there are many patched potholes, but these only make for a bumpy rather than a dangerous ride. Given the few options for safe, traffic-free bicycling in Maryland, most of us are willing to put up with an uneven pavement.

Trip Description

Begin your visit with a required stop at the contact station on Bald Eagle Drive. Obtain a written permit for your use of the area; it must be carried with you at all times. The staff is friendly and enthusiastic and will explain your options and give advice. There are wheelchair-accessible bathrooms here as well as drinking water and trash cans.

There is one important rule to be observed on the North Tract of the Patuxent Research Refuge. Should you find ammunition of any kind, report—but do not touch—any such ordnance. The surrounding forests and fields may still contain unexploded ammunition of various sorts and sizes that could detonate if handled or stepped on. Decontamination of the property has occurred on an annual basis since 1991, but there is no guarantee that every shell has been or ever will be found. Although it is unlikely that you will find unexploded ordnance, it still happens from time to time, so for your own safety, obey all the rules.

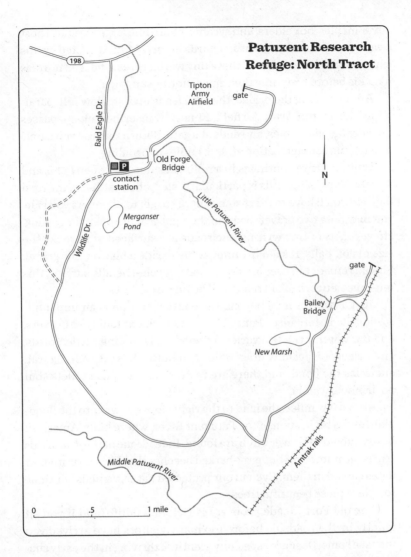

Mounting your bike, leave the parking lot at the contact station and turn left on Wildlife Drive. The road passes through the typical local forest of mixed hardwoods and pines. Few of these trees are old or large, indicating that the land was once more open than it is now. After 0.4 mile, a bridge crosses the Little Patuxent River. This coastal plain riparian habitat is one of the nicest natural areas on this ride. From the bridge, look for great blue herons, mallards, wood ducks, and kingfishers on the water in all seasons. The streamside silver maples, box elders, and sycamores are fine large trees and host a variety of tropical migrant songbirds in early May. Attracted by this expanse of unbroken forest, these tiny warblers rest and feed in areas like this before resuming their migration at sundown.

After crossing the bridge, the road leads up a shallow hill, paralleling the Tipton Army Airfield. Finally, it inscribes a loop, passes the Fort Meade stables, and ends at a gate. Return the way you came, passing the contact station after 3.4 miles of pedaling.

Wildlife Drive continues in a rolling fashion past open fields and forests. None of the hills is particularly steep, but neither is the road flat, and you'll have to exert some energy to get up them. As you ride, you may note two gravel roads on the right that are open for cycling. However, as of this writing, the roads are surfaced with rocks the size of golf balls. It's almost impossible to ride a bike on this gravel. Should refuge staff ever provide a more bicycle-friendly surface, this ten-mile network of old roads will be fun to explore.

Just a quarter mile beyond the contact station is an impoundment called Merganser Pond. There is a resident family of beavers, and the water attracts a variety of wildlife, including turtles, birds, and insects (especially dragonflies and butterflies). A walking trail encircles the pond, and there are restrooms with flush toilets (but no drinking water).

After a few miles, the land to the right slopes down into the floodplain of the main stem of the Patuxent River, where holly, American beech, tupelo, and river birch are found. Indeed, one of the joys of this trip is the number of big, gray-barked beeches that have no initials or dates carved in them. Even in our protected parks, vandals continue to deface these beautiful trees.

The old Fort Meade property is rich in wildlife, and if you sit quietly by the roadside before too many visitors have arrived you may see some. Deer are especially plentiful, thriving in the early successional stages and at the edges of fields. In order to control this population and to provide recreational hunting opportunities, the Fish and Wildlife Service permits bow, black powder, and shotgun hunting September through January. Other mammals present include beaver, mink, raccoon, muskrat, otter, mice, shrews, voles, and rabbits. A pair of bald eagles nest on the center property, successfully fledging young each year.

At mile 5.1 (from the contact station), New Marsh appears on the left. This shallow pond is filled with wetland plants. Perhaps the most interesting are bladderworts, aquatic plants that capture insects and are especially abundant in this wetland. The only part of a bladderwort above the water is the flower, which in this species is yellow and about six inches in height. Below the waterline, feathery leaf-like structures both support the plant and perform photosynthesis. Located along these stems are the "bladders," tiny traps that capture water fleas, mosquito larvae, protozoa, and similar small aquatic animals. Each trap has trigger hairs that, when contacted, cause an inrush of water into the bladder, sweeping the prey in along with the liquid. This entire process can occur in as little as a few hundredths of a second. Enzymes are then secreted into the bladder; these digest the animal, releasing nutrients for the bladderwort's use.

As you near the end of Wildlife Drive, re-cross the Little Patuxent River at Bailey Bridge. Emerging from the heart of the Patuxent Research Refuge, the river looks pastoral and inviting. The floodplain, where the rich alluvial soil accumulates, has a fine collection of wildflowers, but, once again, for safety's sake, view them from a distance—with binoculars from the bridge. Just beyond Bailey Bridge is a pretty little marsh filled with cattails and a dense collection of wooden duck boxes. All too soon the road ends at a gate; return the way you came. The distance from the contact station to this gate and back is 12.5 miles.

Directions

From Washington or Baltimore, take the Baltimore-Washington Parkway (I-295). Exit at Route 198, turning east. Go 1.8 miles and turn right onto Bald Eagle Drive. Continue 0.9 mile on this dirt road to the contact station.

Other Outdoor Recreational Opportunities Nearby

The South Tract of Patuxent Research Refuge has a modern visitor center, and several hiking trails leave from this focal point.

VULTURES

Look up to the sky almost anywhere in rural areas of Maryland and you stand a fair chance of seeing one of our most common but least-loved birds: a vulture. Soaring on unseen thermals and air currents, seemingly without effort, the vulture looks down with haughty disdain on all of our activities, sure and confident that they will yield his next meal. Vultures are scavengers and carrion feeders; they actually provide an important service in recycling dead animal material.

There are two species of vultures in Maryland: turkey vultures and black vultures. Turkey vultures (often referred to as TVs by birders) are the larger of the two, with a wingspan of up to six feet. In the sky, they are easily differentiated from other large birds by the long duration of time between wing flaps and the set of the wings at a dihedral angle above the horizontal. TVs also seem to rock back and forth unsteadily as they soar. At closer distances, the trailing edge of the wings is seen to be lighter in color, the wingtips fingerlike, the tail narrow, and the head small and red in color. Black vultures are smaller and chunkier birds, with a maximum wingspan of less than five feet. They have a wider tail and wings, white may show at the wing tips, and they have black heads. Because of their less efficient aerodynamic shape, black vultures have to flap much more frequently between bouts of soaring.

During most of the year, vultures roost communally in dead or sparsely leaved trees, often with a southeastern exposure so as to facilitate warming in the morning's first rays of light. These roosts can be quite large; one in Talbot County numbered over 500 birds, who in addition to perching on trees settled on rooftops, windowsills, and automobiles. In spring, breeding pairs disperse to find nesting sites, the most favored of which are in tree cavities, under cliff overhangs, and in dense scrub. Between one and three eggs are laid, and the young are tended by both parents. Although predators no doubt take a toll on nestlings, the repulsive vulture habit of projectile vomiting deters most human disturbance.

Turkey vultures locate dead animals primarily by using their sense of smell. Research has shown that a fresh kill is often ignored by TVs, as is extremely rotten meat; a certain amount of decay is necessary to release odors, whereas too much can endanger the bird by introducing heavy bacterial loads into the meal. Black vultures, on the other hand, locate food primarily by sight, often keeping visual track of turkey vultures.

Baltimore/Washington International Airport (BWI) Trail

Section: Airport circuit
County: Anne Arundel
Distance: 10.1 miles; circuit ride
Type: Multi-use recreational trail
Surface: Asphalt
Difficulty: Easy to moderate. Some rolling hills, some flat
Hazards: Vehicular traffic at road crossings
Highlights: Close views of aircraft, some pockets of nature
More Information: Anne Arundel County Department of Recreation and Parks, (410) 222-7317
Street Address: 7 Amtrak Way, BWI Thurgood Marshall Airport, Maryland 21240 (MARC train parking garage); 740 Elkridge Landing Road, BWI Airport, Maryland 21240 (Elkridge Landing Road roadside parking)
GPS Coordinates: 39.192325, 76.694385 (MARC train parking garage); 39.191342, 76.680194 (Elkridge Landing Road roadside parking)

Encircling Baltimore/Washington International Thurgood Marshall Airport is a well-used and thoroughly enjoyable 10.1-mile asphalt, multi-use recreational path known as the BWI Trail. A popular feature of this trail is the Thomas Dixon, Jr., Aircraft Observation Area, where jets landing on the airport's main runway roar past, close enough and low enough to see the faces of passengers peering out the windows. While the BWI Trail has little to offer in terms of nature, it is a valuable recreational resource close to the homes of

68

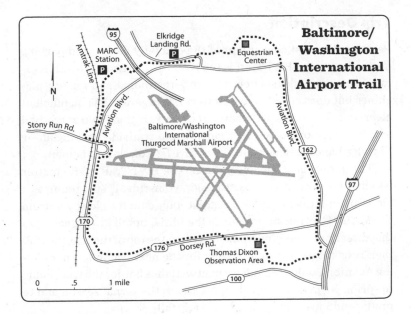

tens of thousands of Maryland citizens. It is popular with families and casual recreational cyclists, but significant numbers of more experienced riders on skinny-tired road bikes also use it, especially for shoulder-season and summer after-work training rides.

The BWI Trail is most often ridden as a circuit, but energetic cyclists can extend their ride by taking a short connector trail that links to the start of the Baltimore and Annapolis (B&A) Trail. From this point, the B&A Trail runs southward for 13.3 paved miles to the outskirts of Annapolis.

A salutary feature of the BWI Trail is its accessibility to public transportation. The BWI MARC train station is located just 100 yards off the trail's northwest corner; the Penn Line connects Union Station in Washington, DC, with Penn Station in Baltimore City, stopping at BWI and several other venues along the route. On weekends, as of this writing, specially outfitted passenger coaches are added to the MARC train that can accommodate bicycles. (No tandems, recumbents, tricycles, mopeds, or bikes with training wheels are allowed.) Bicycles are also permitted on Baltimore's Light Rail line (on a space-available basis); the Light Rail ends in the airport terminal, adjacent to a branch of the BWI Trail.

Trip Description

Perhaps the most convenient of the officially designated parking areas serving the BWI Trail is the BWI MARC/Amtrak station garage, which provides sheltered parking, restrooms, and vending machines but does charge a fee. However, this garage has insufficient clearance for bikes carried on a roof rack. If that is your method of bike transport, consider roadside and trailside parking along Elkridge Landing Road as an alternative (see directions below).

The garage is at the low point on the BWI Trail, so no matter which direction you choose to begin your ride, it still requires a blood-pumping pedal uphill. I suggest going counter-clockwise from the MARC/Amtrak station, since the initial uphill is a bit easier in that direction. Emerging from the trees at the top of the rise, the trail then runs mostly flat and straight for the next two miles, paralleling Aviation Boulevard. A few small wetlands border the trail, home to spring peepers and wood frogs early in the vernal season and to pretty wildflowers in summer and early fall.

At the intersection of Dorsey Road and Aviation Boulevard, the trail turns ninety degrees to the left, now running in an easterly direction. The next mile is mostly uphill, although never too steeply, crossing a few wooden bridges, with the fenced airport property on one side and busy Dorsey Road on the other. Just beyond the crest of the hill is the first of several road crossings, each eased by traffic lights and pedestrian crossing signals.

Just ahead is the Thomas Dixon Aircraft Observation Area. While this could be an alternative parking area to access the BWI Trail, it is usually quite crowded, with lines of cars waiting like vultures for someone to leave. Its attractiveness is due to the dramatic views of jets as they approach the landing strip at BWI Airport. BWI is a busy airport, and as soon as one plane roars by, the lights of the next one in the queue are visible. There is a popular playground here, and families often picnic while watching planes land.

Over the next mile, the trail winds its twisting way through a forest of Virginia pines and small oaks. A few American hollies and mountain laurels form the shrub layer, brightening the winter forest. The sandy soil supports several kinds of mosses, some lichens, and in places a patchy ground cover of club mosses. These primitive vascular plants do not flower but spread by runners and through airborne spores. In the nineteenth century, the spores were collected and when lit by a match provided a flash of illumination for photography. The evergreen scale-like leaves are sometimes used in winter holiday wreaths.

As the trail emerges from the forest, it takes another ninety-degree turn, now heading north. At Stewart Avenue, note the signs indicating a fork. To the right is the John Overstreet Connector Trail, which runs for 1.3 miles through Sawmill Creek Park, reaching a junction with the start of the Baltimore and Annapolis (B&A) Trail. Bear left to continue on the BWI Trail.

At a stoplight, use the pedestrian crossing signal to carefully traverse Dorsey Road. The trail now runs between Aviation Boulevard and the airport fenceline through a mostly open terrain of mowed lawns, ornamental trees and shrubs, and plantings of sun-loving native wildflowers. On the far side of the road are two gas stations with restrooms and snacks available for purchase.

Ahead is the historic Benson-Hammond House, a large three-story brick home dating from the 1820s. It is maintained as a museum by the Ann Arrundell County Historical Society and is often open for tours on weekends. Now on the National Register of Historic Places, this was the only structure spared demolition when the State of Maryland purchased 3,200 acres in 1947 for what was to become Friendship Airport.

From the Benson-Hammond House, the remaining three miles form the hilliest portion of the BWI Trail. The path first crosses Aviation Boulevard at a traffic light with a pedestrian crossing signal. Just beyond this is a swampy pond that often hosts red-winged blackbirds, great blue herons, and sunning turtles. Rising uphill, the pathway crosses Camp Meade Road, runs alongside Lindale Middle School, and reaches the Andover Equestrian Center, where horses often graze next to the trail. Another quarter mile brings you to the highest point on the BWI Trail, a breezy open hilltop where the entire airport complex is visible.

From here, an enjoyable coast downhill leads to a crossing of Elkridge Landing Road, where convenient roadside parking is always available. This intersection also marks the point where a branch trail leads to the airport terminal and Baltimore's Light Rail public transportation system. The final mile on the main trail continues to be rolling but is mostly downhill; the circuit finishes within view of the MARC/Amtrak station.

Directions

From either the Baltimore or Washington, DC, Beltways, take I-295 south or north, respectively. Take exit 2 onto I-195, following signs for BWI Airport. Then take exit 1B onto Route 170 and turn right at the second stoplight, Amtrak Boulevard. This road leads to the MARC/Amtrak station. For alternative parking along Elkridge Landing Road, get off I-195 at exit 1A, turn left at the first traffic light, then left again at the next light; park at the bottom of the hill.

Other Outdoor Recreational Opportunities Nearby

The BWI Trail links with the B&A Trail; see the text for directions. Patapsco Valley State Park has many hiking trails and one loop suitable for cycling; the Avalon section of the park is about a ten-minute drive from BWI.

PARKING LOT GULLS

Winter brings an incongruous sight to shopping mall parking lots: flocks of medium-sized gulls, loafing, resting, and occasionally squabbling over discarded scraps of human food. What brings these gulls to suburban parking lots, so distant from their usual coastline haunts?

Most parking lot gulls are ring-billed gulls, a common and widespread species that winters along the East, West, and Gulf Coasts, and into the Mississippi Valley. With a catholic diet, ring-bills have found landfills and garbage dumps to be a plentiful source of food when their summer provender of insects and earthworms fails. However, other animals, including predators like foxes and peregrine falcons, are also attracted to dumps and landfills, so ring-bills depart for safer locales between bouts of feeding. Parking lots are flat and open, where predators can be easily and promptly sighted, and harassment, save by the occasional reprobate motorist, is minimal. In snowy weather, mall parking lots are promptly cleared to blacktop so the birds don't have to stand in snow. On sunny days, that same blacktop absorbs heat and provides a much warmer surface than grass, dirt, or concrete. Finally, many such parking lots are brightly lit at night, improving visibility and discouraging owls.

Ring-bills are by far the most numerous gull found in parking lots. As their common name implies, a blackish band encircles the bill near the far end. Adult ring-bills have white bodies and yellow feet, with pale gray wings tipped with black. Juveniles have gray or brown streaks on the head and body, with a black band on the tail.

Ring-billed gulls display a variety of behaviors that can be readily studied by a patient observer. Most interactions between gulls occur during squabbles over food. Threat behaviors include head bobbing, open-wing charges, and even physical contact like pecking and wing-pulling, but by far the most common threat behavior is the aggressive display. The bird lowers his head to his feet and extends his body while calling and raising his head to shoulder level. Appeasement displays include assuming a hunched posture accompanied by high-pitched cries, and head flagging, where the head jerks away from an opponent.

By April, ring-bills leave Maryland for nesting grounds in southern Canada and the northern tier of states west of the Great Lakes. Here they nest in colonies on the ground, usually on islands where four-legged predators are absent. While the hemispheric population is now several million birds, persecution by humans between 1850 and 1920 made the species uncommon.

The next time the winter blahs get you down, remember that relief is as close as your nearest mall parking lot, where ring-billed gulls display some fascinating behaviors for you to observe from the warmth of your car. Be sure to bring your binoculars and a favorite bird identification guide, too, since other species of gulls, including the occasional rare vagrant, sometime loaf with their ring-billed relatives. For example, a black-headed gull once frequented the parking lot at Hunt Valley Mall for at least two winters.

Anacostia Riverwalk Trail

Section: Bladensburg Waterfront Park to Anacostia Riverwalk and return
County: Washington, DC
Distance: 18.7 miles as described; circuit ride
Type: Mostly off-road, multi-use recreational trail, a few lightly traveled roads
Surface: Asphalt
Difficulty: Easy, but with a few short hills
Hazards: Traffic at road crossings
Highlights: Riparian forest, urban parks, Anacostia Riverwalk development
More Information: District Department of Transportation, https://ddot.dc
.gov/page/anacostia-riverwalk-trail, (202) 673-6813
Street Address: 4601 Annapolis Road, Bladensburg, Maryland 20710
(Bladensburg Waterfront Park)
GPS Coordinates: 38.933371, 76.938000 (Bladensburg Waterfront Park
trailhead)

Prejudices are hard to overcome. Say the name "Anacostia" or the phrase "east of the river" and some Maryland and DC residents think only of urban blight and crime. Cycle the Anacostia Riverwalk Trail, however, and you'll find a delightful ride through beautiful scenery on a paved multi-use trail system that continues to be developed and improved. The section near Kenilworth Aquatic Gardens opened in November 2016 and within days became a valued route for bike commuters, connecting Capitol Hill with the Maryland suburbs. More casual riders will appreciate the sinuous curves here that make cycling this portion of the trail a delight. Downriver, the well-kept lawns of Anacostia Park reveal expansive views of the DC skyline to the west. The Anacostia Riverwalk itself, near the Washington Nationals baseball stadium, is a trendy area of new residences, shops, and restaurants with a bike-friendly boardwalk and eye-catching

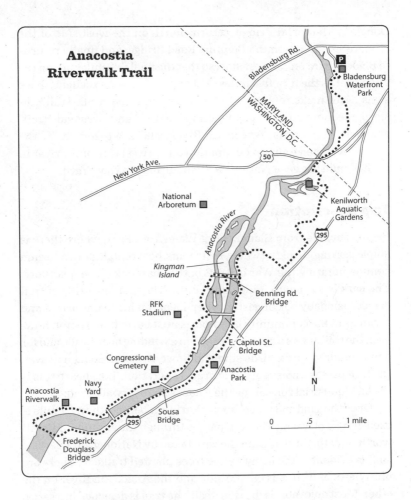

Anacostia
Riverwalk Trail

Bladensburg Rd.

P

Bladensburg
Waterfront
Park

MARYLAND
WASHINGTON, D.C.

New York Ave.

50

National
Arboretum

Anacostia River

Kenilworth
Aquatic
Gardens

295

Kingman
Island

Benning Rd.
Bridge

RFK
Stadium

E. Capitol St.
Bridge

Congressional
Cemetery

Anacostia
Park

N

Anacostia
Riverwalk

Navy
Yard

Sousa
Bridge

0   .5   1 mile

295

Frederick
Douglass
Bridge

public art. It's hard to imagine a more scenically varied ride, and somewhere along the way, any preconceived notions about "Anacostia" will drop away like autumn leaves.

Washington, DC, residents have a variety of places to access the Anacostia Riverwalk Trail within the city limits, and enough familiarity with the area to locate those access points. Maryland residents, however, will find Bladensburg Waterfront Park to be a convenient starting point, since it is only a mile from the Baltimore-Washington Parkway (I-295). From here, the ride described is in the shape of the lower case letter "d." Riding south from Bladensburg, the trail runs down the east side of the Anacostia River, crosses it on the Frederick

Douglass Memorial Bridge, returns north on the west side of the river, re-crosses it on the Benning Road Bridge, and finally returns to Bladensburg on the east side, so that the final five miles are on the same trail as the first five miles. Although signage is excellent, those signs never make reference to the "Anacostia Riverwalk Trail"; instead, the more specific terms "east side trail" and "west side trail" are used. The words "Anacostia Riverwalk" are reserved for the newly developed tourism destination on the west side of the river in the half mile between Nationals Stadium and the Navy Yard.

Trip Description

Begin your ride from Bladensburg Waterfront Park, where there is ample parking, drinking water, restrooms, boat rental, and a museum commemorating the War of 1812 battle that took place near here. The park is open daily, dawn until dusk. The first few yards of trail can occasionally be congested when local rowing teams arrive and organize at the community boathouse. Just beyond this point, however, the trail enters a riparian forest on a winding boardwalk, and for a few hundred yards, birds sing and flowers bloom. Soon, however, the trail passes a noisy sand and gravel operation. Take heart: this is the last industrial zone along the Anacostia Riverwalk Trail.

Once the sand and gravel operation is left behind, the next mile is exceedingly pleasant. The trail passes through the grounds of Kenilworth Aquatic Gardens, and the care taken by National Park Service staff is evident in the many native trees planted trailside. There are nice views of wetlands on one side and the Anacostia River on the other. Most enjoyable is the ride itself; the trail is designed in a series of sweeping curves that make cycling it a true delight. Kenilworth Aquatic Gardens is well worth a visit should you wish to detour from the trail. Signage will guide you to the entrance, which is not on the Anacostia Riverwalk Trail itself.

All too soon the trail leaves the river and enters Kenilworth Park, where there are extensive athletic fields and open space. Beyond this point, the trail detours into a residential neighborhood for about a half mile. One lane of a two-lane road has been closed to vehicular traffic and dedicated to cycling, with a physical barrier separating the two. It feels safe, even for children on bikes, since traffic is sparse on this residential road. Eventually, a dedicated bike trail resumes.

At mile 5.2 from Bladensburg Waterfront Park the first major trail junction is reached. A sign for "west side trails" directs you across the Benning Road Bridge in the event you wish to ride the remaining trails in a counter-clockwise direction. However, the description below is for a clockwise circuit, so follow the sign for "east side trails."

Another mile of pleasant riding delivers you to Anacostia Park, where restrooms and drinking water are available. The broad lawns of this urban park lead down to the shores of the Anacostia River, now contained by a low seawall. Gulls wheel overhead, sometimes loafing on low tide mud flats within easy viewing distance. Great blue herons and kingfishers make forays down to this point from the wilder parts of the Anacostia upriver. Perhaps surprisingly, beavers are present here as well in this urban setting; all the trees in the park have wire mesh wrapped around their lower trunks to discourage beavers from chewing on the inner bark of these trees.

In less than another mile, follow the trail over the Frederick Douglass Memorial Bridge on a dedicated bike lane separated from traffic by a retaining wall. Once on the west side of the Anacostia, the Washington Nationals baseball stadium is directly ahead; turn right on Potomac Street and enter the magical world of the Anacostia Riverwalk. This large public space is bordered by luxury apartments, restaurants, and shops. There are plazas, boardwalks, and footbridges, with sculptures, gardens, water features, and benches scattered about in a fashion pleasing to the eye. It's a popular place, inviting the cyclist, walker, or tourist to tarry a while and enjoy the scene.

Proceeding north, the trail passes into the Washington Navy Yard, with a brick pavement underfoot and a sturdy wrought-iron fence separating you from the neat buildings and grounds. Bike riding is prohibited here, so dismount and walk your bike for the half mile of waterfront covered by the Navy Yard. Just beyond the north gate, cross Martin Luther King, Jr., Boulevard at the only at-grade street crossing of this ride.

The next mile is a curious mix of old and newly developed bike trail. Most of it is on a beat-up road that only exists to service several lightly used marinas along the Anacostia; this section is scheduled for an upgrade. In contrast, a new (and no doubt expensive) bridge over railroad tracks hints at what the trail will be like in the future.

One of the more interesting sights on this stretch of trail is Congressional Cemetery. Opened in 1807, this cemetery is permanent home to many elected officials who died prior to the Civil War. For much of the twentieth century, the cemetery was neglected, a trash- and weed-filled place that was to be avoided. By the 1990s, however, local residents began to remove debris, cut the grass, and plant flowers and shrubs; soon the old cemetery once again became a reputable place. The variety of both old and new monuments is amazing; you, too, can be buried here (for a fee) in this historic cemetery.

The next item of note along the trail is RFK Stadium, dramatic of architecture but somehow looking a bit frowsy. Built in 1961, RFK is now considered obsolete, and there are plans to tear it down, with options to then redevelop the campus.

At the north end of the RFK campus is a side trail leading to two islands in the Anacostia River, Heritage Island and Kingman Island. Heritage is small and low, flooding with some frequency, while Kingman sits well above the high-water mark. Bicycles are permitted should you wish to explore these isles.

Within 100 yards is the Benning Road Bridge; use it to cross the Anacostia to the east bank. (There are no bike paths north of Benning Road on the west side of the river, and no other crossings of the Anacostia.) Rejoin the Anacostia Riverwalk Trail and use it to cycle 5.5 miles back to the Bladensburg Waterfront Park.

Directions

From the Baltimore/Washington Parkway (I-295), take Route 450, Annapolis Road, west. Go 1.3 miles and turn left into Bladensburg Waterfront Park.

Other Outdoor Recreational Opportunities Nearby

To the north of Bladensburg Waterfront Park is a network of multi-use recreational trails that lead to a variety of neighborhoods. It is covered in this book as the Anacostia Tributary Trail System. The National Arboretum is also nearby, and cycling through the grounds (described elsewhere in this book) is an excellent way to enjoy its many botanical treasures.

TOP TEN NON-NATIVE PLANTS YOU SHOULD REMOVE FROM YOUR PROPERTY

You may have noticed that in this book I often mention non-native plants and note locations where you might see them. My hope is to raise your consciousness regarding non-native plants so that you can take steps to eliminate them from your own property, or from public property like parks, forests, and reserves. Non-native plants often displace native plants, thus affecting the diversity, stability, and resilience of the environment we share. Most parks now host programs where citizens can learn how to identify key invasive non-native plants and then work in the field to remove them. I commend these to you; contact your favorite local park for schedule information. Removing non-native plants in your local park is actually a fun activity for the whole family, and leaves you with both a feeling of accomplishment and a sense of civic pride. So what are some of plant species that are both non-native and invasive?

1. **Porcelainberry.** This vine is exceedingly common in central Maryland, growing quickly and forming sheets of stems and leaves overtop of native vegetation. It eventually kills

(continued)

whatever it grows on by blocking sunlight and removing nutrients and water from the soil. The leaves of porcelainberry look a lot like the leaves of wild grape, with 3–5 palmate lobes. It can be distinguished from grapevines by examining the stem pith (white versus brown for grape), the bark (grapevine bark shreds, while porcelainberry bark does not), and both the shape and color of the berries. Porcelainberry fruits are shiny, vary in color from blue to purple on the same stem, and are held upright; grape fruits are uniformly purple when ripe and hang in clusters. While porcelainberry vines may be cut and pulled off whatever support they are growing on, the only way to truly kill the plant is to paint undiluted glyphosate (an herbicide) on the very recently cut stem.

2. **Lesser celandine.** This herbaceous ground cover grows abundantly in alluvial soils, forming dense mats that choke out native wildflowers like bloodroot, spring beauties, toothwort, and trout lilies. The leaves are shiny and the flowers are bright yellow, superficially similar in form to dandelion. Lesser celandine is a perennial, but only appears above ground in March, April, and May. The use of herbicides to control lesser celandine is problematic since desirable native wildflowers are more susceptible to the herbicide and will also be killed. Further, I have found glyphosate painted on the leaves to be ineffective. Manual removal works, but the top five inches of soil must be excavated, and every lesser celandine bulb removed by hand. Clearly, this method is practical only for small patches in the home garden. Elimination of lesser celandine from local parks is virtually impossible, and I am unaware of any programs attempting to do so.

3. **English ivy.** This common and beloved vine of gardens and walls is far less benign when it escapes to our forests. Here, the robust vine can grow up to one hundred feet tall, its roots attaching firmly to the tree's bark. Branches spread several feet from the trunk, and the combined weight of stem and evergreen leaves can pull down a weakened or dying tree. Fruits are dark purple, almost black, in color, and are eaten by birds, who pass the still-viable seeds in their waste. Fortunately, English ivy is fairly easily controlled when it grows

on trees. Clip out and remove a six-inch segment of every ivy vine around the entire circumference of the tree, being careful to remove the tiny roots as well. The ivy leaves above the cut will die and fall off within a few years.

4. **Oriental bittersweet.** A climbing vine, Oriental bittersweet is fairly inconspicuous until late autumn, when its distinctive red seeds encased in yellow pods stand out against the gray forest. Originally brought to America to be used in Christmas wreaths, this vine is spread when the seeds are eaten and dispersed by birds. Oriental bittersweet forms loose tangles that can eventually kill the host tree. Control by applying glyphosate to the freshly cut stem.

5. **Japanese barberry.** This small shrub forms a dense, spiny bush that displaces native vegetation, alters soil chemistry, and tolerates drought and heavy shade. White-tailed deer avoid it, so barberry spreads rapidly in heavily overgrazed forests. It has attractive red foliage and plentiful red berries in autumn. Research has shown barberry is a common refuge for deer ticks, who favor the increased humidity that accumulates inside the foliage. Japanese barberry can be removed manually as long as care is taken to remove all the roots. Regrettably, Japanese barberry is still sold in some plant nurseries.

6. **Japanese knotweed.** This ornamental shrub can attain a height of up to twelve feet and form thickets twenty feet in diameter. It grows vigorously, tolerates a wide variety of soil types and moistures, and responds to cutting by sending up shoots from its extensive root system. The roots spread both horizontally and vertically and can crack concrete, asphalt, mortar, and the packed clay of embankments. The only way to control Japanese knotweed is to paint concentrated herbicide on the recently cut stem.

7. *Phragmites.* This tall grass with a leafy inflorescence grows in wetlands, from extensive freshwater marshes to roadside drainage ditches. It grows so densely that nothing else can grow with it, and on disturbed mud flats it is often the only plant present. It has little value for wildlife, whereas the

(continued)

marsh plants it displaces (cattails and wild rice) are especially valuable to birds and small mammals. It can be controlled by first burning and then treating with an herbicide, although treatments usually must be continued for two or more growing seasons to be effective.

8. **Garlic mustard.** An annual herbaceous plant less than two feet tall at maturity, garlic mustard grows in April and May, competing with and displacing native wildflowers. Garlic mustard secretes antifungal chemicals into the soil, disrupting fungi that grow in a symbiotic association with plant roots. Unlike many invasive plant species, it is easily controlled manually. Merely pull the stem upward; the roots usually come along. Make sure, however, that you do so before any seedpods form, or you'll have to do it again the next year.

9. **Asiatic tearthumb.** Also known as mile-a-minute vine for its rapid growth, the recurved barbs along the stem of this spreading vine make it difficult to remove manually. It grows as a sheet over shrubs and tree seedlings, preventing photosynthesis to the extent that the host plant may even die. Attractive blue berries are produced in quantity and spread by birds, deer, and even ants. The seeds are self-pollinating, profuse in number, can float for a week, and may persist in the soil seed bank for up to six years. Low-growing plants can be controlled by mowing, but herbicide may be needed for tearthumbs fully entwined with its host.

10. **Kudzu.** A perennial vine associated with the southeastern states, kudzu reaches its northern geographical limit in Maryland. It grows very quickly, smothering whatever it grows on by shading the leaves of the host plant. Kudzu seems to grow better than other invasive vines on power lines and abandoned houses. In the summer, fragrant purple flowers are conspicuous. The extensive root system of a kudzu plant can weigh up to 400 pounds. Kudzu prefers full sun but does not successfully invade fields with cattle, who eat the plant quite readily. Herbicides like glyphosate typically require multiple treatments over several years to recently cut stems to be effective.

Assateague ponies. The feral horses of Assateague are surely the most beloved animals on the island, but they can be aggressive pests when seeking food in the campgrounds.

Northern flicker. This conspicuous noisy woodpecker sometimes forages on the ground. The red malar (moustache) marks this as a western member of the species. Among many other places, look for flickers along the Washington, Baltimore, and Annapolis Trail.

Yellow-crowned night-heron. These large water birds nest in small colonies at only a few places in Maryland. Surprisingly, these rookeries are in urban areas like along the Jones Falls in Baltimore City and Sligo Creek in Takoma Park. Their primary food is the pollution-tolerant and very common crayfish, which may explain the night heron's presence at these locations.

Buttercups (*facing page*). Nothing says "spring" so much as a field of blooming buttercups. While lovely to look at, the plant is toxic to horses and cattle. Look for buttercups in April in fields along the C&O Canal towpath and the Three Notch Trail.

Sugar maple leaves. Sugar maples are our most brilliantly colored autumn tree as their leaves change. They are most often found in the western part of Maryland at higher elevations. The Great Allegheny Passage is well known for its fall color, in large measure owing to lots of sugar maples.

Cross Island Trail (*facing page*). Spanning the width of Kent Island, the Cross Island Trail links a scenic bayfront park with the restaurants and bars of Kent Narrows, passing through pockets of natural beauty along the way.

Coyote. Coyotes may be North America's most adaptable predator. Despite being shot, trapped, and poisoned, coyotes have recolonized Maryland and are now found in every county of the state. Coyotes are most often seen at dusk; their scat is common along the Chesapeake and Delaware Canal Trail.

Turkey vulture. Turkey vultures are our most frequently seen soaring bird. They eat carrion; their featherless heads reduce their bacterial load. Look up almost anywhere in Maryland to see a TV, as birders call them; turkey vultures rarely flap, and hold their wings in a shallow V-shape.

Dunker Church, Antietam National Battlefield. This humble structure, a symbol of love and peace, was in the midst of the battle of Antietam on September 17, 1862. Immediately after the battle, it was used temporarily as a medical aid station. In 1962, on the one hundredth anniversary of the battle, the church, which had been moved, was restored on its first foundation using as much of its original materials as possible.

Monarch butterfly (*facing page*). Our most brilliantly colored common butterfly, monarchs are still frequently seen throughout Maryland. Their numbers are declining, however, due to loss of their obligate food plant, milkweed. September along the Western Maryland Rail Trail and the Cross Island Trail are good places to see monarchs.

National Arboretum and capitol columns. A bicycle tour of the lightly traveled roads of the National Arboretum is the perfect way to get around this off-the-beaten-path Washington, DC, gem. There's lots to see at every season, but when 60,000 azaleas bloom in early May, there is no finer venue to cycle and walk.

Anacostia Riverwalk Trail (*facing page*). This Washington, DC, paved recreational trail has it all: a section that features superb natural beauty, portions whose effortless curves are a joy to ride, wonderful views of our nation's capital city, and a passage through Riverwalk, DC's hottest new renewal area, complete with upscale shops and enticing restaurants.

Eastern meadowlark. Once common birds of grasslands, meadowlarks have lost a quarter of their nesting habitat in Maryland since 1987. When you find one, it is a joy to hear their liquid, warbling songs echoing over grassy meadows. Meadowlarks are often observed at Blackwater National Wildlife Refuge.

Red-headed woodpecker. An uncommon bird in most of Maryland, this woodpecker's entirely red head makes identification easy and certain. The Indian Head Trail is a likely location for spotting red-heads.

Eastern bluebird. These companionable, gentle birds were once uncommon in Maryland, but their population recovered nicely when we humans began setting out nesting boxes for their use. Antietam National Battlefield has a well-monitored bluebird trail, although most of the recreational trails in this book host nest boxes.

Virginia bluebells (*facing page*). Found in alluvial soils along many Maryland rivers, Virginia bluebells flower before trees leaf out, and their leaves die back by early summer. The C&O Canal towpath and Patuxent Research Refuge host extensive displays of bluebells each April.

BWI Trail. Encircling Baltimore/Washington International Airport, the BWI Trail permits close views of jets as they land and features several fun-to-ride short rolling hills and the relaxing scents of a pine forest.

Anacostia Tributary Trail System

Section: Section 1: Northeast Branch Trail
    Section 2: Paint Branch Trail
    Section 3: Northwest Branch Trail
    Section 4: Sligo Creek Trail
Counties: Prince George's, Montgomery
Distance: Section 1: 3.0 miles one way
    Section 2: 3.5 miles one way, with a 1.4-mile loop extension
    Section 3: 7.0 miles one way
    Section 4: 10.2 miles one way
Type: Multi-use recreational trail
Surface: Asphalt
Difficulty: Easy to moderate. Mostly flat or slightly rolling with one hill on
    the Sligo Creek Trail in Takoma Park
Hazards: Traffic at road crossings, heavy pedestrian use within the University
    of Maryland campus
Highlights: River valley forests, pleasant suburban scenery
More Information: Anacostia Watershed Restoration Partnership,
    www.anacostia.net; Friends of Sligo Creek, www.friendsofsligocreek
    .org; Wheaton Regional Park, www.montgomeryparks.org/parks-and
    -trails/wheaton-regional-park, (301) 495-2595
Street Address: Sections 1 and 3: Bladensburg Waterfront Park, 4601 Annap-
    olis Road, Bladensburg, Maryland 20710
    Section 2: Lake Artemesia Natural Area, 8200 55th Avenue, Berwyn
    Heights, Maryland 20740
    Section 4: Wheaton Regional Park, 2000 Shorefield Road, Silver Spring,
    Maryland 20902
GPS Coordinates: Sections 1 and 3: 38.933758, 76.937818 (Bladensburg
    Waterfront Park)

Section 2: 38.981837, 76.920246 (start of Paint Branch Trail just south of
Lake Artemesia)
Section 4: 39.053052, 77.043804 (Shorefield Road entrance, Wheaton
Regional Park)

The Anacostia River drains a substantial portion of western
Prince George's County inside the Capital Beltway (I-495). The
region is almost entirely suburban, with a high population density
and consistently heavy traffic on most roads. However, the county
had the foresight to purchase much of the land bordering the Anacostia's feeder streams, creating a palmate network of green spaces
populated with playgrounds, ballfields, grassy lawns, and pocket
woodlands. And through these connected parklands runs almost
twenty miles of asphalt-paved, off-road, multi-use recreational trails
enjoyed by cyclists of all abilities.

Four distinct but linked trails are described, using the nomen-
clature of Prince George's County Department of Parks and Recreation. Like branches of a tree, all arise from the central trunk, in
this case the Anacostia Riverwalk Trail. This trail is mostly located
in Washington, DC, proper and is described in the previous chapter
of this book. About 1.5 miles of the Anacostia Riverwalk Trail extend into Prince George's County near Bladensburg, and that town is
used as the point of origin for the Anacostia Tributary Trail System
descriptions.

The Anacostia Tributary Trail System is marked in two ways.
Square wooden posts, about two feet high and close to a foot wide,
are found at almost all trail junctions. The trail name is inscribed in
the wood, but the paint has mostly worn away, so be sure to check the
wording. In addition, the asphalt surface of the trail has lane divide
dashes painted in a different color for each named trail, although
again time has weathered the paint to the point where some are almost invisible.

Be forewarned: restrooms are a rare commodity on the entire
Anacostia Tributary Trail System, so begin your ride with an empty
bladder and a full water bottle.

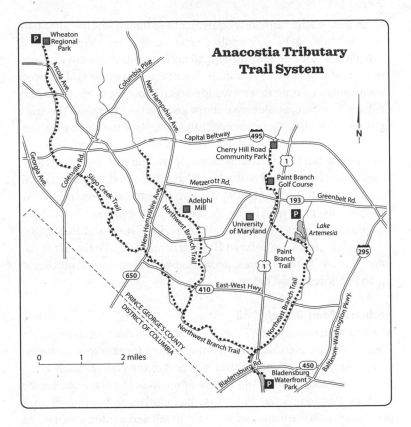

Trip Description

Section 1: Northeast Branch Trail

From Bladensburg Waterfront Park, begin your ride by cycling in a northerly direction. The Waterfront Park is a popular location for rowing clubs loading, unloading, and launching sculls, but within 100 yards upstream, the Anacostia becomes too shallow for these delicate watercraft. Indeed, the fall line, the final set of mild rapids before tidewater, can be seen from the trail about one mile upriver from Bladensburg. This point marks the northern terminus of the Anacostia Riverwalk Trail, which here diverges into the Northeast Branch Trail and the Northwest Branch Trail.

Bear right to get on the Northeast Branch Trail, with yellow lane-divide dashes. For the first 1.5 miles, the trail occupies a berm about a dozen feet above a large, flat meadow bordering Northeast Branch.

(A "branch" is approximately equivalent to a "creek" in size, although the term "creek" generally implies a steeper gradient.) This artificial floodplain, built and maintained to accommodate transient large volumes of stormwater runoff, is maintained in grass and mowed episodically to eliminate any woody vegetation that might grow and capture flood debris. Because there are no trees to shade the trail here, it can be a hot, though mercifully brief, place to ride in summer.

At Riverdale Road, an at-grade road crossing, the trail enters a more typical landscape of tree-shaded parkland with intermittently spaced playgrounds and ballfields. It continues in this fashion until its terminus at about mile 3 at the entrance to Lake Artemesia. At this point, the pavement forks. To the right is the Indian Creek Trail, which at just a mile in length is not described; it ends at Route 193, Greenbelt Road, in the Berwyn Heights community. To the left is the Paint Branch Trail, which follows that watercourse for another 4 miles and is described below.

Section 2: Paint Branch Trail

The southern origin of the Paint Branch Trail is reached through the Lake Artemesia Natural Area, a popular park for strolling, running, and birding. Although not technically part of the Paint Branch Trail, the 1.4-mile loop around the lake is often cycled by those riding for exercise. Restrooms and water may be found on an isthmus of land protruding into the center of the lake. In fall and winter, a variety of ducks frequent Lake Artemesia, and birding during spring migration can be rewarding. Begin your ride from the Lake Artemesia parking area at the north end of the lake (near the intersection of 5th Avenue and Berwyn Road).

The area near Lake Artemesia was the site of an African American community called Lakewood during the first half of the twentieth century. De facto segregation in housing was the rule in Maryland at this time, so Lakewood gave African American families a place to live near their work at the nearby University of Maryland campus. Most of the families were displaced in the 1960s as the housing underwent "urban renewal," the Metro railbed was built, and Lake Artemesia was drained and physically relocated. In the past century, Prince George's County has changed from a place where people of color were a small minority to today, where 63 percent of the county at the last census were black and 15 percent were hispanic.

The Paint Branch Trail is accessed from the southern end of the paved trail around Lake Artemesia. Turn right, north, and follow the trail signs. The mile of trail between Lake Artemesia and the University of Maryland is often crowded with students walking, running, and cycling. Cross busy Route 1, Baltimore Boulevard, then take the pedestrian bridge over Paint Branch, and finally bear right, following the light blue lane-divide dashes of the Paint Branch Trail. Eventually leaving the campus behind, the trail skirts Paint Branch Golf Course. This area was severely impacted by a tornado in 2001 and is slowly recovering. Virtually all the large trees were felled, so the vegetation trailside is mostly fast-growing small trees, shrubs, and dense tangles of vines and other undergrowth. Many are non-native and invasive; eventually, saplings of native trees like oaks and tulip poplars will grow large enough to shade out these aliens, but that will take several more decades.

Four miles from its origin, the Paint Branch Trail reaches its northern terminus at Cherry Hill Road Community Park, within sight and sound of the Capital Beltway.

Section 3: Northwest Branch Trail
The Northwest Branch Trail is 7 miles in length, described from its origin at the Anacostia Riverwalk Trail one mile north of Bladensburg and ending near the Capital Beltway (I-495), in Montgomery County. The lane-divide dashes are red.

The Northwest Branch Trail begins at the same point as the Northeast Branch Trail, so be sure to properly read the trail marker. The first five miles pass through and are bordered by ballfields, playgrounds, and open space, often with houses visible. This is an old trail, and there are many cracks and heaves in the asphalt where tree roots have undermined the pavement. The trail goes under several major roads; these pinch points are often narrow, with tight turns, so use care and go slowly at these locations, especially on weekends when more people use the trail. Another feature of the Northwest Branch Trail that is unusual is that rather than bridging drainage ditches and seep springs, the trail dips into the swale. After a heavy rain, use care if there is more than an inch of water in such troughs.

At Adelphi Mill, a beautiful restored stone building, the trail enters a shallow gorge. The slopes are covered with trees that shade the path, and Northwest Branch now burbles and dashes over rocks, creating the sound of water music. Birds sing, and civilization is seemingly left far behind. For those interested in scenic beauty and nature, this may be the best portion of the entire Anacostia Tributary Trails system. After two miles of such pleasant riding, the trail ends at Oakview Drive. There is a rough trail suitable for determined hikers beyond this point in a northerly direction; within a few hundred yards, the Capital Beltway (I-495), soars far overhead on an arched concrete bridge.

Section 4: Sligo Creek Trail

The westernmost tributary of the Anacostia, Sligo Creek is scenic but the trail is heavily used. It boasts an active "Friends" group that watches over and maintains its 10.2 miles. This trail also has the most elevation change of any in the Anacostia Tributary complex, although it will require only one or two gear changes on the uphills. The Sligo Creek Trail has lane-divide dashes painted in purple, although this color has weathered so that it blends almost perfectly with the surrounding asphalt.

Because there is no major trailhead at the southern end of the Sligo Creek Trail, it is described from its terminus in Wheaton Regional Park to its end where the trail joins the Northwest Branch Trail. Begin your ride from the parking lots at the Shorefield Road entrance to Wheaton Regional Park. There are restrooms, drinking water, picnic tables, and a seasonal snack bar here, but the major attraction is the miniature railroad, which operates in warmer weather. The asphalt trail departs from the far end of the southernmost parking lot, skirting the railroad tracks before entering the forest. At a T intersection, turn right, continue for a few hundred yards, and then turn right again at the next trail junction. This brings you out onto Nairne Avenue. Go three blocks on this quiet residential street, then turn left on Ventura Avenue. If all this seems confusing, just follow the signage.

The Sligo Creek off-road, multi-use recreational trail actually begins at the end of Ventura Avenue. Initially, the path runs through an unremarkable wooded area surrounded by pleasant residential neighborhoods. At mile 2.6, pass under the Capital Beltway (I-495), near Holy Cross Hospital.

Another two miles of enjoyable riding on a curving path that links many small parks, playgrounds, and picnic areas brings you to Piney

Branch Road and the border of the town of Takoma Park. Takoma Park is a charming suburb with small-town character; it is one of the most desirable places to live in the Maryland suburbs of Washington, DC. Sometime known as the "People's Republic of Takoma Park" for the left-leaning political views of many residents, Takoma Park cherishes Sligo Creek, and the trail is busy at all hours with people walking for exercise, strolling with children and dogs, and cycling for fun and commuting.

It's a narrow valley in Takoma Park, and it is shared by the trail, the creek, and a busy road, Sligo Creek Parkway. The three inter-twine in a complex fashion, and a notable feature of this next two-mile section is the eleven plank and steel arch bridges that permit the trail to cross and re-cross Sligo Creek.

Although water quality in Sligo Creek is not the best, the valley contains a surprisingly diverse assemblage of creatures. Volunteers have identified 45 species of butterflies, 68 kinds of breeding birds, and more than 350 native plant species. Among the more surprising regular residents are black-crowned night herons, moderately large wading birds that often stand immobile for long periods waiting for their favorite meal, crayfish, to amble past on the creek bottom.

At Washington Adventist Hospital, Sligo Creek's gradient steep-ens, as does the adjacent trail's. It's an exhilarating ride downhill to the far end of Takoma Park and New Hampshire Avenue. Cross this busy road with care. The remaining two miles of the Sligo Creek Trail are more typical of the other trails in the Anacostia net-work, relatively flat and passing through neighborhoods of smaller houses with less impressive landscaping. At mile 10.2 from Whea-ton Regional Park, the Sligo Creek Trail merges with the Northwest Branch Trail.

Directions

Sections 1 and 3: To reach Bladensburg Waterfront Park, take the Baltimore/Washington Parkway (I-295) south from the Capital Belt-way (I-495). Exit the Parkway at Annapolis Road, Route 450. Go 1.3 miles and turn left into Bladensburg Waterfront Park.

Section 2: To reach Lake Artemesia Natural Area, take exit 23, Kenilworth Avenue, off the Capital Beltway (I-495), heading south. Go a short distance on Kenilworth Avenue and turn right, west, on Greenbelt Road, Route 193. In less than one mile, turn right on Branchville Road. Branchville Road becomes Ballew Avenue, and then becomes 55th Avenue. Proceed to the end and park.

Section 4: To reach Wheaton Regional Park, take exit 31, Georgia Avenue (Route 97) north off the Capital Beltway (I-495). Go about 3 miles and turn right on Shorefield Road. Proceed to the end and park.

Other Outdoor Recreational Opportunities Nearby

The Anacostia Riverwalk Trail begins at Bladensburg Waterfront Park and is a fine place to cycle or stroll. The National Arboretum is also nearby. Both trails are described elsewhere in this book.

WHAT'S SO GREAT ABOUT NATIVE PLANTS? AND WHAT'S SO BAD ABOUT NON-NATIVE PLANTS?

In this book, I often write about plants you might see on your rides. Some are native; some are not. What's the big deal about native versus non-native plants? Why are native plants so beneficial for our Maryland ecology? Why are non-native plants so detrimental? And most importantly, why should you care?

First, what's the difference between a native and a non-native plant? In general, native plants have grown in the area under consideration for at least several hundred years. In Maryland, that's an easy call; if a plant was here prior to colonization by European settlers, it's native. Ah, but wait: bald cypress trees have grown in Maryland for millennia, but only on the coastal plain, the counties east of Interstate 95. If you find a bald cypress growing well to the west, it was probably planted there by some well-meaning gardener or arborist. So would you call that bald cypress a native tree when you find it along a stream near Frederick, Maryland? If you say yes, would you change your answer if I told you that tree will never reproduce, never form cones? How about tamarack trees? In Maryland, they are only found natively in Garrett County, at high elevations, growing in frost pocket bogs. Yet there is a stand of tamaracks in Baltimore County, in Gunpowder State Park. Native, or non-native?

The answer to this question is not found in taxonomy but in ecology. All organisms interact with other organisms in their environment. For example, native plants have co-evolved with specific kinds of fungi and insects. Some orchid species cannot live after being transplanted because the new soil lacks the proper kind of fungus that aids the orchid in the uptake of nutrients through the roots. Some flowers are shaped such that they can be pollinated only by certain species of insects; if transplanted where those insects are missing, the plant will not be able to reproduce. So a plant is native only where it has grown since precolonial days, and where it grows in the proper context with its biotic and abiotic environment. It must be able to live, successfully reproduce, and persist over time.

But why are native plants so much more beneficial than non-natives? The simple answer is that native plant species have more relationships with other kinds of organisms that share their environment. More relationships mean more diversity, stability, and resilience for the ecosystem.

One example is the ubiquitous wetland plant *Phragmites*. It tends to take over freshwater marshes that have been disturbed, replacing native plants like wild rice and cattails. Although *Phragmites* has been in the Chesapeake region for about 300 years, it supports just 5 species of phytophagous insects, whereas in its native Europe, more than 170 kinds of insects feed on its leaves. *Phragmites* grows so densely that many birds and small mammals that live in the marsh are displaced. So *Phragmites* reduces the diversity of plants and animals of its marshland habitat, and that in turn can affect the ability of the ecosystem to respond to changes like disease and sea level rise.

Another example is the American chestnut tree. A century ago, the chestnut was a common forest tree in Maryland. It produced an abundant nut crop every year, unlike oaks, which produce large crops of acorns approximately every third year. Thus, in lean acorn years, animals like gray squirrels, white-tailed deer, and red-headed woodpeckers still had a reliable source of winter

(*continued*)

food, ensuring a higher annual rate of survival. When chestnut blight killed virtually every American chestnut tree, the eastern forest was left a less biodiverse place, more susceptible to other kinds of diseases and insect infestations.

"But, really . . ." I hear you say. "Who cares? Why should I care?" Perhaps an analogy will help. Consider an airplane, and from it you begin removing bolts, at random. Remove a few bolts, and probably the plane will still fly. Continue removing bolts, however, and eventually the plane will break apart in flight. Or, early on in the process of removing bolts, you remove one that is more critical than most of the others, and the plane crashes. Species of native plants and animals are like the bolts, and the environment is like the airplane. Remove enough native species, or the wrong critical native species, and the environment starts to collapse. And furthermore, we don't know in advance which bolts, which native species, are the critical ones. The only prudent course of action is to keep all the bolts, all the native species, so that the plane, and the environment, continue to function in an optimal fashion.

Rock Creek Trail and Beach Drive

Section: Section 1: Upper Rock Creek Trail: Washington, DC, Border to
Lake Needwood
Section 2: Beach Drive (weekends and holidays only)
Section 3: Lower Rock Creek Trail: Peirce Mill to the Potomac River
County: Section 1: Montgomery
Section 2: Washington, DC
Section 3: Washington, DC
Distance: Section 1: 14.4 miles one way
Section 2: 4.7 miles one way
Section 3: 4.3 miles one way
Type: Sections 1 and 3: Multi-use recreational bike trails
Section 2: Park road closed to most traffic on weekends
Surface: Asphalt
Difficulty: Sections 1 and 2: Easy to moderate. Rolling terrain
Section 3: Easy. Flat
Hazards: Section 1: Some sharp turns, road crossings, short hills
Section 2: Occasional cars, steady elevation change
Section 3: Narrow, crowded trail with adjacent heavy traffic
Highlights: Forested river valley, large, old trees, historical sites, the
National Zoo
More Information: Montgomery County Parks, http://montgomeryparks
.org/parks-and-trails/rock-creek-stream-valley-park, (301) 495-2595;
Rock Creek Park, https:// nps.gov/rocr/index.htm, (202) 895-6000.
Street Address: 7901 Meadowbrook Lane, Chevy Chase, Maryland 20815
(Meadowbrook Park); 2401 Tilden Street NW, Washington, DC
(Peirce Mill)

GPS Coordinates: 38.985280, 77.059702 (Meadowbrook Park); 38.940280, 77.051858 (Peirce Mill)

The District of Columbia and surrounding counties boast a complex of off-road, mostly paved bicycle trails that is the envy of other metropolitan areas. It is possible, for example, to park your car in the distant suburb of Rockville, Maryland, mount your bike, and pedal downtown to visit such world-class attractions as the National Zoo, the Lincoln Memorial, and the Kennedy Center. By crossing the Potomac River, you can cycle south to visit Mount Vernon, George Washington's home. Or you can pick up the C&O Canal towpath in Georgetown and pedal 184 miles west to Cumberland. And with all this mileage, you will not have to share a single yard with automobiles (although, unavoidably, there are a number of intersections to be crossed). In addition, the Metro, Washington's subway system, provides access to these trails at several points. (Bicycles are allowed on the Metro on weekends, holidays, and during off-peak times on weekdays.)

The Rock Creek Trail is one of the best of these paths. Originating north of the city in the still expanding Gaithersburg-Rockville biotech corridor, the Rock Creek Trail follows its namesake stream for 23 miles, winding through a leafy, cool greenway. Furthermore, it provides access to downtown without the hassles of driving through city and tourist traffic. To the first-time visiting cyclist, it is nothing less than amazing to emerge from a fastness of tall trees and flowing water to see the Washington Monument in the distance and the Kennedy Center just down the road.

The Rock Creek Trail is best divided into three sections. The upper trail runs from just north of Rockville to the city line and is the least crowded. At this point, the official bike trail leaves the valley and is rarely used. Instead, Beach Drive, which parallels the creek and is closed to traffic on weekends, constitutes the second section of the trail. Finally, the off-road bike trail picks up again at the terminus of Beach Drive near Peirce Mill and runs downtown to the Potomac River near Foggy Bottom and Georgetown. Each of these sections has its own charm, and each is well worth a visit.

Trip Description

Section 1: Upper Rock Creek Trail: Washington, DC, Border
to Lake Needwood

The upper portion of the Rock Creek Trail follows the Rock Creek stream valley for a distance of 14.4 miles. This segment of the Rock Creek Trail is shaded by a canopy of large trees and follows a greenbelt of small recreational and picnicking parks. Unlike Washington's part of the trail, it is less manicured, but in some places has suburban houses in sight beyond a "beauty strip" of trees. The upper Rock Creek Trail is a valuable resource, for in few places has there been enough foresight to set aside so many miles of undeveloped corridor for recreation and re-creation.

This trail is described running northward from a starting point near the Washington, DC / Montgomery County border, because most cyclists who arrive in this area use I-495, the Capital Beltway. There is ample parking along Beach Drive just north of the city line in several roadside lots. Public stables operated by the National Capital Parks and Planning Commission are found in this area, called Meadowbrook Park, and offer riding lessons to children. Just beyond are a picnic area (with shelters), trash cans, bathrooms, playing fields, and an extensive playground known as Candy Cane City.

From here, the designated bike trail closely follows Rock Creek in a northerly direction through a lovely neighborhood of big, well-kept houses. At mile 2.3, the trail passes under I-495; the Mormon Temple, a well-known local landmark, is visible just up the hill. The trail now turns west for a mile, passing under busy Connecticut Avenue; this underpass, like another at Norbeck Road and an overpass at Veirs Mill Road, is a real (but expensive) boon to cyclists. For the next several miles, the trail is in good shape, having been repaved recently. (The northern half of the Rock Creek Trail has an uneven surface with many cracks and heaves owing to tree roots.)

This trail is not flat. It winds over small hills that on occasion are steep and require standing on the pedals. The section between Winding Creek Park and Dewey Park, mile 5.5 to 6.5, is especially hilly. In addition, the trail has a number of sharp turns, some located on hills that make proper control of the bicycle a must. Be courteous to fellow cyclists and pedestrians and yield the right-of-way whenever possible.

The upper Rock Creek Trail is heavily used by the local community, especially on weekends and in the evening. Expect to see lots of kids, strolling couples and families, and a scattering of joggers. As with virtually all trails, visit on a weekday for a more solitary experience.

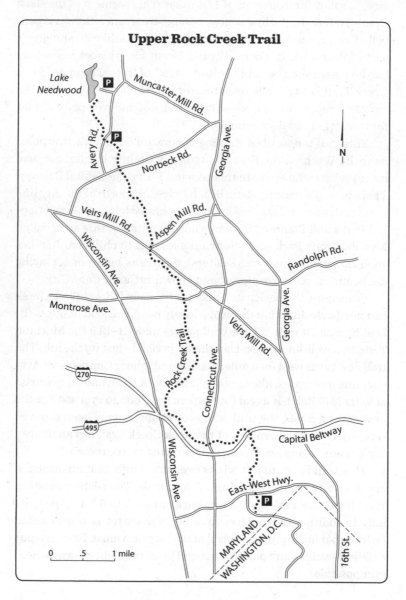

Upper Rock Creek Trail

The Rock Creek valley in Montgomery County is a shallow one. Few dramatic outcrops of rocks or cliffsides are seen, in contrast to the fall line gorge below Military Road in the District. The bike trail passes through several forested habitats. River bottom forest is more common in the upper reaches of the trail, where low river-banks allow floodwaters to spread out among the tree boles. Most of the lower sections of the trail pass through a mixed mesophytic forest of modest proportions. These are mature but not really large trees on a soil of moderate moisture content—sort of the "silent majority" of forest habitats in the Maryland Piedmont. Finally, significant portions of the trail border or dissect recreational lands, complete with tot lots, tennis courts, soccer fields, and the like. Most or all have water available (except in winter) and have one or more portable toilets.

The final, northernmost mile of the Upper Rock Creek Trail is most pleasant, with a remote, bucolic feel to the surrounding forest. After the trail's steepest uphill stretch, it ends at Lake Needwood. Administered by the National Capital Parks and Planning Commission, Lake Needwood is a popular picnic site and can be crowded during the summer. Fishing is allowed (with the proper Maryland license) in the lake, although swimming and boating are not. The Rock Creek Trail terminates at the south end of the lake, where parking for 100 cars, water, trash cans, and bathrooms are available.

Section 2: Beach Drive

On weekends and holidays, a remarkable transformation overcomes Beach Drive, a busy artery that normally funnels traffic into and out of downtown DC. The National Park Service closes 4.7 miles of Beach Drive to motorized traffic from 7 a.m. to 7 p.m., on Saturdays and Sundays so that walkers, joggers, cyclists, and in-line skaters can have unhindered use of both lanes. Such an unusual and insightful decision has been a real benefit to cyclists of all ages and abilities, and the public has responded by making Beach Drive a popular weekend destination. Fortunately, there is plenty of room for all because the road is so much wider than a typical bike path. If you're slow, or merely busy looking at the scenery, just keep to the right. Note, however, that Beach Drive has no shoulders, funnels high-speed traffic downtown on weekdays, and is never used by any sane cyclist Monday through Friday.

This trip begins at the point where Beach Drive is gated to vehicles, just inside the city line. Several parking lots line Beach Drive north of here; just pick any one that has available space. All are associated with tall trees shading the picnic tables and grassy play areas of Meadowbrook Park.

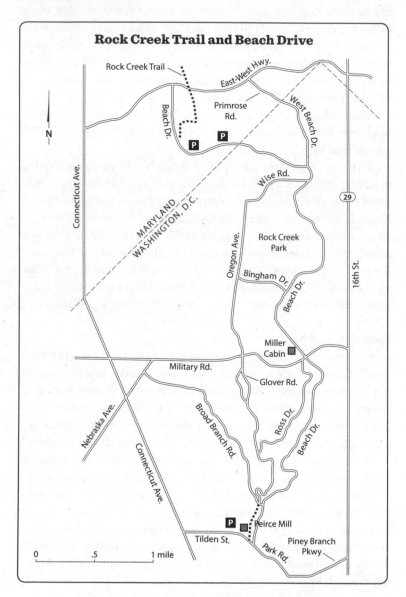

Rock Creek Trail and Beach Drive

The upper reaches of Rock Creek Park are downright beautiful. The park is almost a mile wide, not just a mere greenbelt (as it is in much of its upper and lower sections). The rolling hills feature well-developed soils that harbor all sorts of mature trees. Birdlife is more common and diverse, since there is space enough for a viable population. Spring wildflower displays are at their best here.

If this first gate is mile 0, a break in the sylvan peace comes quickly, at mile 0.6. Vehicular traffic is allowed between here and Wise Drive, a few hundred yards south. Use care in this short stretch, although drivers are usually courteous to cyclists. The next three miles are a pure delight, as the road winds through the shady coolness, always within the sound of flowing water in Rock Creek. In summer, this is a most pleasant place, as the temperature is frequently 10° cooler than in the surrounding city streets; this is the place to go for an early morning ride on those steamy, humid summer days.

At mile 2.4, the Miller Cabin appears on the west side. Home to Joaquin Miller, a prominent poet who lived here in the 1880s, it is the site of summertime poetry readings. Just south of here, the path crosses busy Military Road. During the Civil War it was an important supply route to the ring of forts protecting the nation's capital.

At Military Road, Rock Creek crosses the fall line, the last set of rapids before the river enters the gravels and sands of the Coastal Plain. Extending downriver for the next half mile, the creek drops dramatically over boulders and through tight chutes. Because the flow of Rock Creek is normally so small, the water will be almost imperceptible, and you can cross the creek by jumping from rock to rock. But when a summer thunderstorm hits Washington, rainwater from a thousand storm sewers dumps into Rock Creek, and the river becomes a roaring, cascading torrent of mud, logs, and other debris. It is an impressive sight.

The rapids cease by the time Beach Drive crosses the river on the aptly named Boulder Bridge. The walls of the bridge are composed of large rounded boulders from Rock Creek. You won't find another bridge like this one anywhere.

At mile 4.4, Broad Branch Road converges with Beach Drive. This marks the end of the closed section of Beach Drive, as the bike path resumes its way southward. Join the bike path for a short 0.3-mile jog to Peirce Mill.

Although Beach Drive is officially closed to traffic, you will encounter the occasional car. A number of reservable picnic areas line most of Beach Drive, and vehicles with permits are allowed access to them.

Section 3: Lower Rock Creek Trail: Peirce Mill to the Potomac River

This 4.3-mile section of the Rock Creek Trail is most notable for its surprising character. As the trail slices through the heart of the city, few cyclists would ever imagine the pulse of urban life going on just beyond the trees that top the valley rim. This would be a very pretty trail even if it were not in the city; its urban nature merely adds utility to its other, not inconsiderable, charms.

There are a few drawbacks to this lower portion of the trail, however. Care must be taken, especially with children, at a number of road crossings. At rush hour, these intersections may be next to impossible to cross; DC drivers are not noted for their courtesy. The path is heavily used, as you might expect, and not just by bicyclists; it is a favorite place for city-dwelling joggers who have few other

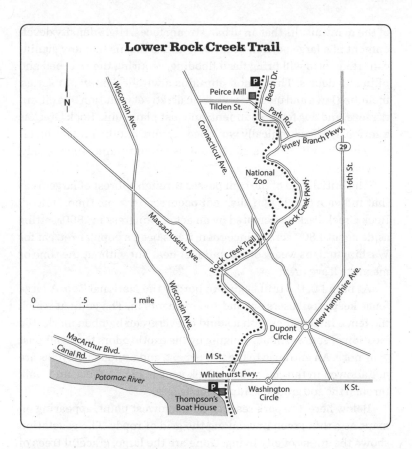

Lower Rock Creek Trail

N

Wisconsin Ave.

Peirce Mill

Tilden St.

Beach Dr.

Park Rd.

Piney Branch Pkwy.

29

Connecticut Ave.

National Zoo

16th St.

Massachusetts Ave.

Rock Creek Trail

Rock Creek Pkwy.

Wisconsin Ave.

0   .5   1 mile

Dupont Circle

New Hampshire Ave.

MacArthur Blvd.

Canal Rd.

M St.

Potomac River

Whitehurst Fwy.

Thompson's Boat House

Washington Circle

K St.

options. Finally, the path is a narrow one, ranging between four and eight feet wide. That's just enough room for two bikes to pass, assuming they're both in control. All of these problems can be avoided by visiting at less popular times, especially on weekdays.

Begin your ride on the lower Rock Creek Trail at Peirce Mill, a restored 1820s-era gristmill. Operated by the National Park Service, which administers Rock Creek Park, the mill uses water power to convert whole grain into finely ground flour. Cornmeal and buckwheat flour are available for sale when the mill is open. Adjacent to the mill is the Art Barn, where local artists display their efforts and conduct classes. Picnic tables, trash cans, portable toilets, and parking for about 50 cars may be found at Peirce Mill.

Leave Peirce Mill, heading southward. The trail continues to follow Rock Creek, a small tributary that has been subjected to most of the many insults that an urban stream faces. High-density development of a large portion of the watershed means that any significant rainstorm will bring flash flooding, scouring the riverbed and piling up debris. This runoff contains a witches' brew of nasties, including lawn and industrial chemicals; street pollution like oil, antifreeze, and dog feces; sediment; and just plain junk. Rock Creek is a seriously and chronically wounded stream, but the protection afforded by its adjacent greenbelt assures its continuing, albeit sickly, survival.

The initial mile of the trail passes through a forest of large trees that indicate that logging has not occurred in some time. Indeed, Rock Creek Park was created by an act of Congress in 1890, setting aside about 1,800 acres. Since then, it has been a popular retreat for Washingtonians weary of the summer heat but without the time or means to leave town.

At mile 1.0, the trail begins to border the National Zoo. A large fence keeps trail users out and zoo residents in. The point at which the fence intertwines with a stand of evergreen bamboo marks the location of some exhibits, judging by the exotic odors that waft past your nose. An entrance to the zoo is next, and although bicycles are not allowed in the zoo, you can lock your bike to a fence and walk through the zoo grounds. Admission is free.

Below here, the park reaches its narrowest point, appearing on maps as a thin green line among the grid of roads. The vegetation shows the stress of city living. Gone are the large, graceful trees of the upper, wider portions of the park; only the hardiest, like *Ailanthus altissima*, hold on. Also known as Tree of Heaven, these exotics originally from Asia thrive in many of our cities, growing in trampled, sun-blasted soil and even through cracks in concrete. Ailanthus is almost impossible to eradicate, and a tree cut back grows all the more vigorously, up to twelve feet in one growing season. In addition to ailanthus, several kinds of non-native shrubs and vines choke out the native vegetation along the creek where sunlight penetrates. At least all of this is green.

At mile 3.2, the trail passes Oak Hill Cemetery. Predating the Civil War, a number of ornate monuments speak of a time when the dead received more honor than they do today. Just beyond the cemetery, the trail passes under a beautiful old pink sandstone bridge. Dozens of gargoyles in the persona of a war-bonneted Indian chief grace the bridge; they are one of the mostly forgotten treasures of this capital city.

The frequency of bridges and intersections on this portion of the trail indicates that the terminus is near. The trail runs as a sidewalk adjacent to busy Rock Creek Parkway for a portion of its last mile, and care must be taken here on the narrow path, with heavy traffic just inches away.

A brick pathway overhung with willow trees at mile 4.1 marks the origin of the C&O Canal towpath. The canal is thoroughly urban in its first few miles, and its worldly character in Georgetown belies the remote rural nature of the rest of the 184-mile towpath.

The Rock Creek Trail ends at the parking lot for Thompson Boat Center. From here, the Watergate Hotel is to your left, with the Kennedy Center just beyond. The Washington Monument peeks over the buildings lining Virginia Avenue, also to your left. Thompson's has parking for 65 cars and rents bikes, canoes, rowboats, small sailboats, and rowing shells. Water and sodas are available; bathrooms are not wheelchair-accessible, being located on the second floor of the boathouse.

From Thompson's, you may want to visit the Mall and the monuments of downtown Washington, DC, or you may return to Peirce Mill by way of the Rock Creek Trail.

Directions

Because of the length of the Rock Creek Trail and the complexity of the roads reaching and crossing it, it is best to refer to the maps for access points.

Other Outdoor Recreational Opportunities Nearby

The C&O Canal towpath originates just a few yards from the end of the Lower Rock Creek Trail in Georgetown. It is possible to explore the Mall and monuments of downtown Washington, DC, on designated bike paths. Canoes and kayaks may be rented from Thompson Boat Center to explore the Potomac River and Theodore Roosevelt Island.

THE BROWN-HEADED COWBIRD: BROOD PARASITE EXTRAORDINAIRE

A winter's day at dusk: the setting sun's rays flare off the bottoms of clouds, setting them ablaze with color. The reflected light suffuses the landscape, lending it a warm glow that belies the season. Across the sky, a column of birds appears, on its way to a nightly roost. The birds pass overhead in a seemingly endless parade, thousands of birds for minutes on end.

These winter flocks are mixed groups of Icteridae, blackbirds and their relatives. In Maryland, they typically include starlings, redwings, grackles, and cowbirds. Of these, the brown-headed cowbird is the most interesting. As its name implies, males have a brown head, and also a black body and a short bill; the birds feed mostly on seeds in the winter.

The brown-headed cowbird is eastern North America's only obligate brood parasite: that is, females do not build nests but instead lay their eggs in the nests of other birds. Cowbird eggs develop faster than the eggs of their hosts and hatch sooner. The young are typically larger than their adopted siblings and so successfully compete for a larger share of the food brought back to the nest. In many cases, the host nestlings die. Thus the host parents expend much time and energy raising a bird of another species, reducing both their own fitness and the future size of their population.

Cowbird parasitism is a problem for songbirds in Maryland and throughout the eastern United States. More than 200 species of birds are parasitized, including many that are uncommon and whose populations have long been declining. Warblers, vireos, and flycatchers seem particularly affected; adult birds rarely recognize cowbird eggs as foreign. For example, one researcher found 100 percent of worm-eating warbler nests on Sugarloaf Mountain in Frederick County to be parasitized by cowbirds. Similar results have been observed for other warbler species on a variety of study sites throughout the east, prompting one biologist to note that some nesting populations are "raising nothing but cowbirds."

Why haven't warblers and other host species evolved to recognize and destroy the eggs of invaders, given the strong selective pressure to do so? Biologists note that the brown-headed cowbird is a native of the midwestern grasslands and prairies. As the eastern forest was converted into farmland, the cowbird's range expanded; it is now common everywhere between the Rockies and the Atlantic northward to the boreal forest of Canada. Warblers may not yet have had enough time to evolve a response to this recent stress on their population. However, other birds, like robins, catbirds, and blue jays, do reject cowbird eggs. One ornithologist notes that these larger birds frequently re-nest if disturbed; warblers are less likely to re-nest, because of either their smaller size or their shorter nesting season.

The last refuge of these wood warblers seems to be large tracts of unbroken forest. Cowbirds, being birds of open fields and edges, mostly parasitize nests near forest borders. Indeed, the farther one ventures into a large tract of forest, the fewer cowbirds are seen and the fewer nests are parasitized. However, these tracts must be exceptionally large to ensure a true refugium from brood parasitism; although a study deep in the interior of virgin forest in the Great Smoky Mountains found no cowbirds, they have been seen in the middle of a patch of forest almost a mile from the nearest edge. Nevertheless, many scientists feel that the single most important factor in the decline of songbirds is the fragmentation of our forests, exposing vulnerable species to the depredations of brown-headed cowbirds and other predators that frequent forest openings. Most ornithologists agree that preserving public land in the largest contiguous blocks possible holds the best chance for conserving dwindling populations of warblers and other migrant songbirds.

The National Arboretum

Section: Arboretum roads
County: Washington, DC
Distance: Variable, depending on route
Type: Lightly traveled roads within the grounds
Surface: Asphalt
Difficulty: Moderate. Rolling to hilly
Hazards: Traffic
Highlights: Flowers, shrubs, trees, National Capitol Columns
More Information: The National Arboretum, http://usna.usda.gov,
(202) 245-2726
Street Address: 3501 New York Avenue NE, Washington, DC 20002
GPS Coordinates: 38.912597, 76.971658 (R Street entrance)

Washington, DC, is a city of contrasts: The capital of the most powerful country in the world, it is home to hundreds of thousands of people, some of whom live in opulent houses in enchanting neighborhoods and others who live in crime-ridden poverty as bad as that in any urban center in America. Its trash-filled streets lie close to fine old parks filled with large trees and a sense of wildness. Finally, it is a magnet for visitors and tourists, who hit all of the must-see museums and monuments while ignoring a number of fine facilities and national treasures. The National Arboretum is one such underappreciated place. Located near the outskirts of the city proper, far from any other tourist meccas, the 444-acre arboretum is visited mostly by metropolitan DC residents as a refuge for relaxation from the bustle and stress of urban life. In most seasons, it is usually uncrowded, and even in winter there are always some beautiful plantings to delight the eye. Over nine miles of paved roads

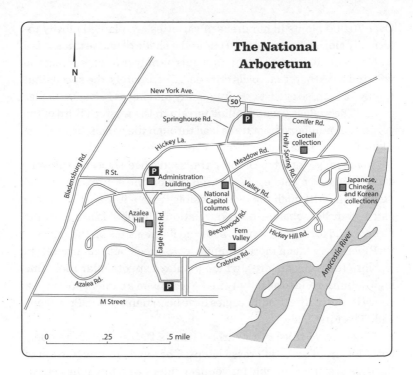

wind gracefully through the gently rolling property, and cycling these lightly traveled paths is a true delight.

Trip Description

Begin your ride from the parking lots just within the R Street entrance. An information center and gift shop are located near here, and bathroom facilities and water are available. Be sure to pick up the arboretum's general brochure; its map provides a key to the location of the many kinds of gardens and vegetation displays.

Because of the aesthetically pleasing but almost random pattern of arboretum roads, no formal bike route is recommended here. Instead, use the map to ride wherever you choose, visiting whatever exhibits hold the most appeal for you. Described here are a few of my favorite gardens and plantings.

Undoubtedly, the arboretum gets the most visitation in late April and early May when its justly famous collection of azaleas blooms.

Over 70,000 plants in hundreds of varieties are planted mostly in-
formally along forest edges and under the shade of native trees. It is a
truly spectacular sight, and this is about the only time of year that you
will find the arboretum roads crowded. Fortunately, the speed limit
is only 15 mph, so cyclists are frequently moving as fast as vehicular
traffic. The azaleas occupy rolling terrain in the western third of the
grounds. A number of foot trails lead through the woods; bring along
a lock for your bike and be sure to stroll these shady paths.

In recent years, a few of these trails have been closed to prevent
disturbance to a bald eagle nest located on the southwest side of
Azalea Hill. Although the nest is visible from a few spots on these
paths, your best chance to see our national symbol is as the adults
fly back and forth between the nest and fishing sites on the Anacostia River. For a much more intimate look, check out the Arboretum
website (dceaglecam.org), which displays spectacular real-time
high definition video of activity in the nest from a camera poised just
above it. Fittingly, the adult eagles have been named "Mr. President"
and "The First Lady."

The central third of the arboretum is flatter and more open,
with dozens of acres of grassy lawns. The roads in this portion of
the park are more suitable for younger riders who might have trou-
ble on the hills elsewhere. Two sites here are especially worth visiting. Dominating the area are the National Capitol Columns. These
historic sandstone columns graced the east central portico of the
United States Capitol from 1826 to 1958, when an addition was built.
The twenty-two columns are a testament to the artistry and skill of
stonecarvers and other craftsmen in the early years of our country.
Not far away is Fern Valley, also worth a stroll on foot. In addition
to a number of ferns, the deeply shaded site along a tiny trickle of a
stream displays a number of native woodland wildflowers. Spring is
the best time to visit here for the most diversity. In the meadow just
outside Fern Valley are many varieties of native wildflowers adapted
to the high light and heat of open land. Summer is perhaps the most
enjoyable time to visit the meadow, when the blooms attract a variety
of insect pollinators.

The eastern third of the Arboretum grounds is dominated by
the informal gardens of the Japanese, Korean, and Chinese collections. Located on a steep hillside overlooking the Anacostia River,
these delightful displays are a wonderful place to enjoy a pleasant

stroll through an exotic landscape. An observant visitor may note that some of these Asian plants bear a striking resemblance to our own North American native flora. During the Pleistocene era, ending about 12,000 years ago, the Bering land bridge connected Asia and North America, enabling some plant species to "move" from one continent to another. Even further back in time, when there was a single continent, Pangaea, trees like ginkos evolved. Once our present continents separated, ginkos became extinct in North America but persisted in Asia to the present. All our North American ginkos descend from seeds and seedlings brought over from Asia during our colonial period.

More fascinating exhibits are located near the administration building. Don't miss the exotic Bonsai collection, perhaps the most popular display at the Arboretum. Some of these miniature trees have been under careful "training" for more than 400 years. Just across the road from the Bonsai exhibit is the national herb garden, a must-see for anyone interested in the culinary and medicinal uses of plants. And if you're an aficionado of almost any other kind of plant, you're likely to find displays of it elsewhere on the arboretum grounds. Enjoy.

Directions

From the Capital Beltway (I-495), take the Baltimore-Washington Parkway (I-295) in toward the city. Exit at New York Avenue, Route 50. At the first stoplight, Bladensburg Road, turn left. Go three blocks, turn left on R Street, and proceed to the arboretum entrance.

Other Outdoor Recreational Opportunities Nearby

Washington, DC, and its surrounding suburbs have a number of surprisingly pleasant bike paths, including the Rock Creek Trail, the Anacostia Riverwalk Trail, and the Capital Crescent Trail. These three trails are described elsewhere in this book.

MEDICINAL PLANTS AND THE VALUE OF BIOLOGICAL DIVERSITY

In the 1970s, far up in the remote mountains of central Mexico, a college student found a very different-looking variety of wild maize. This significant discovery turned out to be a previously unknown species of corn, *Zea diploperennis*. This newly discovered species proved to be resistant to several diseases, and more important, it is the only variety of corn that is perennial rather than annual. *Zea diploperennis* could be worth billions of dollars because it provides a potential source of genetic information that can be transferred into domesticated varieties both by standard breeding methods and by new techniques in molecular biology. The little patch of corn covered less than 25 acres and was slated to be destroyed within a week when it was discovered.

In addition to being the basis for a significant part of our diet, plants have been the source of most of our medicines. About 80 percent of these medicines were originally plant-based, and even today about 30 percent include plant products. Aboriginal cultures have long used plants as remedies for health problems, but even in the United States only a fraction have been scientifically investigated.

The reason for this has as much to do with the prejudices of science and scientists as with anything else. In colonial times, much of medical practice was quackery, embraced by rascals with no training or scruples. Plant extracts were often prescribed as remedies and cures, but the few kernels of truth in herbalism were often obscured by much nonsense. The doctrine of signatures, a holdover from medieval times, is one such quaint example. The doctrine held that God had put plants on earth for mankind's use and had left on each plant a physical clue as to how it might best be used. For example, the woodland wildflower hepatica, with its purplish color and three lobes, resembles the human liver and was thus thought to be useful for liver-related ailments. Although a few of these signatures were fortuitously correct, most were not. As scientific medicine evolved in the mid-nineteenth century, doctors understandably ignored herbalism as mere folklore. Today, we are reexamining plants for their usefulness in medicine.

Among the flora of Maryland are several medically useful species:

- The common woodland plant mayapple contains podophyllin, an anticancer drug.

- Extracts of bloodroot also have antitumor activity.

- Paw paw trees contain biologically active compounds called acetogenins that are under investigation for their effectiveness in cancer therapy.

(continued)

- The active ingredient in aspirin was originally isolated from willow twigs.
- The heart drug digitalis comes from foxglove, a forest wild-flower that has now been naturalized.
- Indian tobacco yields lobeline, a muscle relaxant, and extracts of the plant are also useful in respiratory disorders.
- Jimsonweed and other members of the tomato family produce hallucinogenic alkaloids.

The list goes on, and it will probably never be complete.

The wild plants of our world, therefore, have an economic value in addition to an aesthetic one. When members of the public question the value of a snail darter or spotted owl, or of a tract of wetland or old-growth forest, it is usually from a position of naiveté. Most of our biological heritage remains unexplored for its utility and must be preserved until such time as it can be. Most bacteria, algae, fungi, lower plants, and obscure classes of animals have never been investigated in this regard. There is general agreement among scientists that a wealth of useful compounds exists in plants and other organisms. For this reason alone, preservation of biodiversity is not a luxury but a necessity that our society cannot afford to ignore.

Capital Crescent Trail

Section: Section 1: Bethesda to Georgetown
　Section 2: Bethesda to the vicinity of Silver Spring
County: Section 1: Montgomery and Washington, DC
　Section 2: Montgomery
Distance: Section 1: 7.1 miles one way
　Section 2: 3.3 miles one way
Type: Multi-use recreational trail
Surface: Section 1: Asphalt
　Section 2: Gravel and crushed stone
Difficulty: Easy
Hazards: Traffic at road crossings
Highlights: Riparian forest, Potomac River views
More Information: Coalition for the Capital Crescent Trail http:// cctrail.org,
Street Address: near 4766 Bethesda Avenue, Bethesda, Maryland 20814
GPS Coordinates: 38.980809, 77.095716 (Bethesda Avenue trailhead)

Transportation planners long ago realized the value of a beltway that circumnavigates a metropolitan area, arcing through the suburbs to connect one outlying district with another. Now bicyclists have their own beltway, or at least a portion of one, on the west side of Washington, DC. The Capital Crescent Trail links Bethesda with Georgetown, running through the diverse suburbs west of the city line and then following the Potomac River into downtown.

The Capital Crescent Trail is yet another old railroad bed that has been converted to recreational use. Originally the Georgetown Branch of the B&O Railroad, it has now achieved a higher calling. A seven-mile section of the old rail line, from Bethesda to Georgetown, was completed as a paved multi-use trail in late 1997 and is described in this chapter. North and east of Bethesda, the trail exists as a crushed stone and gravel path, extending just over three miles to the vicinity of Silver Spring. This section of the trail is known as the Georgetown Branch Interim Trail until it is upgraded with asphalt paving, but signage indicates it is part of the Capital Crescent Trail too. Both segments are managed by Montgomery County Department of Parks and Planning in association with the National Capital Parks and Planning Commission.

Trip Description

Section 1: Bethesda to Georgetown

Begin your exploration of the Capital Crescent Trail in downtown Bethesda, where there are several parking lots (where a fee may be charged) near the trail's origin at Bethesda and Woodmont Avenues. A variety of services are available here, including restaurants, snacks, shops, and a popular bookstore. Follow the crowds to the start of the trail on the south side of Bethesda Avenue.

Leaving the urban nature of downtown Bethesda, the trail soon transports you into a cool, leafy green corridor. While this scrim of trees provides only an artificial sense of isolation from nearby neighborhoods, it is enough to make the ride pleasant. In the first mile or so, the trail crosses Little Falls Parkway at grade, where caution should be exercised, and bridges at Bradley Boulevard and River Road. A bit farther, at the Massachusetts Avenue bridge, hikers and cyclists have the option of detouring onto the Little Falls Hiker-Biker Trail, which runs parallel to the Capital Crescent Trail for almost a mile.

That this area has experienced damage and disturbance to its ecology is evident in the kind of plant species lining the trail. Although there are many tall native trees here, shrubs, vines, and herbaceous plants are typically non-native, weedy invasive species. Most obvious are the curtains of vines festooning everything below thirty feet.

Perhaps the most common vine along the Capital Crescent Trail is porcelainberry, a woody, non-native perennial plant that grows vigorously, especially in full sun. Whole hillsides are covered with this climbing vine. Porcelainberry may smother and kill the trees and shrubs upon which it grows. Leaves have a rounded base, three pointed lobes, and prominent veins; by autumn tiny fruits ripen from green to blue or purple.

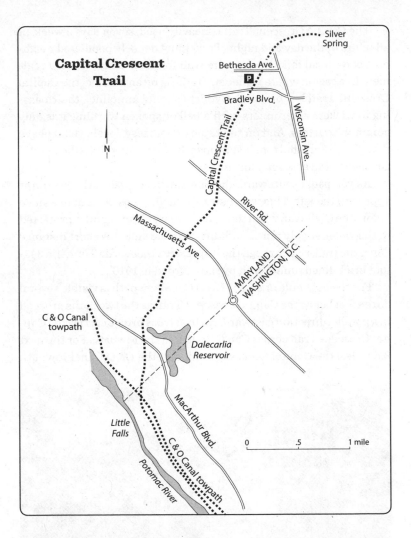

Capital Crescent Trail

Silver Spring

Bethesda Ave.

Bradley Blvd.

Capital Crescent Trail

Wisconsin Ave.

N

River Rd.

Massachusetts Ave.

MARYLAND

WASHINGTON, D.C.

C & O Canal towpath

Dalecarlia Reservoir

Little Falls

MacArthur Blvd.

C & O Canal towpath

Potomac River

0   .5   1 mile

Kudzu is also common here. An Asian species brought to the United States more than 100 years ago, kudzu spreads like wildfire, especially in the southern states where winters are warmer. Recognize kudzu by its leaves, which consist of three shallowly lobed leaflets. Flowers are purple and fragrant, abounding in late summer. Southerners joke that if you throw a kudzu seed over your shoulder, you'd better run, or the vine will catch you as it grows. It's not far from the truth; kudzu can grow up to a foot a day and as much as sixty feet in a year.

The Capital Crescent Trail is heavily used, seven days a week, at all hours of the day and night. Traversing densely populated neighborhoods, local folks flock to the trail for their daily exercise regimen. In a region where vehicular traffic is often snarled, the Capital Crescent Trail is a blessing. Cyclists should announce their passing to walkers and runners with a bell or spoken warning; it is only common courtesy. And on the topic of courtesy, local cyclists have thoughtfully created repair stations with air pumps along the Capital Crescent Trail at several locations.

As you pedal southward, the open lawns of Dalecarlia reservoir appear to the left. This water storage facility has been in use since before the Civil War, when the guns of nearby Fort Sumner protected it, the water supply pipes, and the Potomac valley. A short distance down the trail, ride through the impressive Dalecarlia Tunnel, a 341-foot brick-lined tunnel built by the railroad in 1910.

For the next mile or so, the C&O Canal towpath is visible several dozen feet below the Capital Crescent Trail as the two paths proceed in a parallel direction eastward. An iron truss bridge carries the Capital Crescent Trail across Canal Road and the towpath. For the next 2.5 miles, the Capital Crescent Trail and the C&O Canal towpath

continue to run parallel, at about the same elevation, and often just a few yards apart. Because the towpath is narrow, eroded, and heavily used inside the District border, this parallel, hard-surface path for bicycle use is especially valuable. The trail is densely shaded by mature trees, making it is a cool place to cycle in the summer heat. A surprising amount of bird life inhabits this forest despite its urban character, attesting to the value of riparian habitat for wildlife. Several small wetlands exist far above the level of the Potomac River, fed by leaks from the C&O Canal. There are excellent views of the Potomac and the church spires of Georgetown when the leaves have fallen.

The Capital Crescent Trail terminates in Georgetown at the quaint facilities of the Washington Canoe Club. Victorian accents to the sagging clubhouse speak of more prosperous days, when flatwater canoeing was among the most popular of pastimes.

Section 2: Bethesda to the Vicinity of Silver Spring
This section of the Capital Crescent Trail, which is also known as the Georgetown Branch Interim Trail, runs in a northeasterly direction from downtown Bethesda, and sees much less foot and bicycle traffic. From Bethesda Avenue, follow the signs for the Georgetown Branch Trail across a major intersection and into a tunnel that runs for almost a quarter mile underneath the large buildings of Bethesda. Note that this tunnel is gated and may be closed after dark.

Emerging into sunlight, the railbed surface changes to crushed stone and gravel as it passes the houses of the Chevy Chase neighborhood. Use care crossing busy Connecticut Avenue at mile 1.5. At this point, note that the trail occupies the sidewalk along Connecticut Avenue for about fifty yards before turning right into the trees. A bike shop is located here, which can be useful if you experience mechanical problems.

After an at-grade crossing of Jones Mill Road, the trail enters Rock Creek Park. A bridge more than eighty feet above the streambed gives cyclists wonderful views of the valley below. At the far end of the bridge, a signed branch trail permits a connection with the Rock Creek Trail. Energetic cyclists should realize this junction allows a circuit ride (weekends only) of almost 22 miles, using the Rock Creek Trail, Beach Drive, the C&O Canal towpath, and the Capital Crescent Trail. It is a superb resource for cyclists.

The Georgetown Branch Trail continues for only another half mile before terminating at Stewart Avenue in a rather dreary neighborhood on the outskirts of Silver Spring.

Directions

From the Washington Beltway (I-495) take Route 355, Wisconsin Avenue, south. In downtown Bethesda, turn right on Bethesda Avenue. Go one block to the trail and its associated parking lots.

Other Outdoor Recreational Opportunities Nearby

As noted above, it is possible to create a 22-mile loop by combining the Rock Creek Trail, Beach Drive, the C&O Canal towpath, and the Capital Crescent Trail (weekends only). All of these paths are suitable for walking as well as cycling, are located nearby, and may be traveled individually.

BIOPOLLUTION

The native flora and fauna of Maryland are a diverse and wonderful collection of organisms, but when a plant or animal makes headlines, it is frequently an exotic species introduced into the state by humans. The new immigrant, whether introduced accidentally or on purpose, invariably gains notoriety as a damaging, unpleasant nuisance. Consider this rogue's gallery of well-known foreign organisms that plague Maryland: crabgrass, starlings, gypsy moths, stinkbugs, snakeheads, and even the HIV virus.

Ecologists have long known about the devastating effects that non-native invading species can have on ecosystems. Their populations, uncontrolled by the normal checks to unlimited expansion—predation, parasitism, competition, and disease— invaders frequently displace native organisms, alter the ecology of the community, and may even cause extinctions. Less well understood are the characteristics that make a place susceptible to invasion in the first place. In general, ecological communities already placed under stress seem to be the most fertile breeding grounds for outbreaks of what is now being called biopollution. These stresses are almost invariably caused by humans: plowing, logging, damming, developing land for housing or industry, eliminating native species, and practicing single-crop farming—all of which lead to habitat loss. In addition, it is usually our activities that introduce new immigrants to these stressed ecological communities, by either transporting exotic species inadvertently over geographical barriers or transplanting them purposely.

Perhaps we should have learned our lesson by now; yet the introduction of exotic flora and fauna goes on apace. The public at large likes exotics; witness the popularity of zoos and aquariums. Crops, ornamental plants, game birds, and fish are regularly stocked into new habitats throughout the United States. For example, there are at least 69 species of exotic fish in United States waters, 158 more that have been stocked outside their native range, and countless transplantations of different genetic stocks within the same species. English ivy is still sold in some garden centers, despite festooning and even killing mature trees in Maryland forests.

The reason for our fascination with exotic biota, of course, is that some introductions are pleasant or useful. For example, Sika deer were introduced into Maryland near the turn of the twentieth century and have flourished in the counties of the lower Eastern Shore. They are a popular game species and apparently do not compete with native white-tailed deer, whose numbers increase every year. Non-native brown trout are regularly stocked in Maryland rivers by the Department of Natural Resources and are a favorite with recreational fishermen across the state. However, brown trout displace native brook trout from many miles of prime stream habitat, pushing them upstream into tiny remote creeks.

Some exotics have both positive and negative qualities, and the jury is still out on them. *Hydrilla* is an underwater flowering plant that colonized the Potomac River below Washington, DC, in the 1980s. It has dramatically increased water clarity and created a world-class bass fishery. However, *Hydrilla* mats are all but

(continued)

impenetrable by boat, and they may be preventing the return of native underwater grasses wiped out by pollution in the 1950s and 1960s. Multiflora rose, popular with game managers because it supplies cover and food and prevents erosion, also aggressively displaces native vegetation.

In general, however, non-native species cause problems. With continued development in Maryland, coupled with the increasing frequency of global travel, we can expect more problems with exotics. Insects are especially troublesome and difficult to control. The wooly adelgid has killed thousands of Maryland hemlock trees in the past two decades, and the emerald ash borer seems poised to do the same with ash trees. The best way to control population outbreaks of exotic pest species is often to deliberately introduce a predator. For example, wasps that prey on gypsy moth larvae were transplanted from the moth's native range in Asia and have successfully controlled yearly outbreaks of the moth in New England to the point that spraying of pesticides has been abandoned. Of course, an introduced predator might itself cause problems, so care must be exercised with its release.

Although scientists and managers remain worried about non-native, exotic species, other introductions continue, inadvertently and on purpose. Unfortunately, the ecology of invader species is not a predictive science, so we cannot tell which of these introductions will be detrimental and in what way. The best course is probably to minimize such introductions and to preserve undisturbed large blocks of land where the stresses that mankind places on the environment are at least minimized. In this way, perhaps we can hold the line against the continuing assaults of biopollution.

Gwynns Falls Trail

Section: Interstate 70 terminus to Carroll Park
County: Baltimore County, Baltimore City
Distance: 7.8 miles one way as described, with an additional 1.3-mile round-trip spur
Type: Multi-use recreational trail, with a short section on a public road
Surface: Asphalt, crushed limestone
Difficulty: Easy. Mostly flat but with a few short hills
Hazards: Traffic at road crossings
Highlights: River valley
More Information: Gwynns Falls Trail Council, www.gwynnsfallstrail.org
Street Address: none (I-70 trailhead); none (Winans Meadow trailhead)
GPS Coordinates: 39.301822, 76.708499 (I-70 trailhead); 39.304404, 76.693618 (Winans Meadow trailhead)

There are many advantages to city living, but access to safe, off-road, recreational cycling trails rarely tops the list. Of late, however, Baltimore City has recognized the recreational and eco-logical value of greenways and has been developing paved trails along both the Jones Falls and the Gwynns Falls ("falls" is a local term for a small river or large stream). The Gwynns Falls Trail begins at the eastern end of Interstate 70, passes through Leakin Park, then occupies a narrow greenway valley through Baltimore's westside neighborhoods, and ends its off-road, multi-use recreational trail character at a city golf course. Beyond this point, city streets form the designated "trail," complete with traffic, row houses, businesses, and fenced industrial complexes, but with no evidence of nature except the occasional bedraggled sidewalk shade tree; this portion of the Gwynns Falls Trail is described no further here.

Neither the Gwynns Falls Trail nor Leakin Park is heavily visited, in part because many citizens are still afraid of criminal activity. Leakin Park, in particular, was once notorious as "the place where they dump the bodies." Since the Gwynns Falls Trail opened in the late 1990s, however, that increase in human presence has discouraged illegal activities, and there is almost never a reason to feel unsafe while cycling. Much of the trail is quite beautiful, overhung by mature shade trees that engender a sense of remoteness unusual inside the city line. Birdsong and the music of flowing water are never far away. So do not be discouraged by its sketchy reputation; give the Gwynns Falls Trail an opportunity to impress you with its many positive attributes.

Trip Description

Begin your ride at the eastern terminus of Interstate 70, where there is plenty of parking in the median between the westbound and eastbound lanes. In the late 1960s planners wanted to connect I-70 with I-83 in downtown Baltimore, routing the highway through Leakin Park and some poor neighborhoods of west Baltimore. Activists successfully blocked creation of this road, a signal achievement for citizens against the power of big government. Hence, I-70 meets a surprisingly sudden and unremarkable end here. There are no facilities at all here, however.

The Gwynns Falls Trail is found on the north side of the highway, a narrow, inconspicuous paved path squeezed between an exit ramp and an often trashy hillside. Coast downhill, where the scenery improves upon entering historic Franklintown. Several old houses, meticulously cared for and built of native stone, grace this charming neighborhood. Unfortunately, there is no room for the trail in this 200-yard segment, so you'll be sharing the narrow road with vehicular traffic. If you have small children, you may want to consider parking and beginning your ride just over a mile eastward, at the Winans Meadow trailhead.

Once through Franklintown, the trail becomes separate from the road and enters the sylvan quiet of Leakin Park. It rises up a small hill, then descends an unusual series of switchbacks that demand care and attention. Once on the floodplain of Dead Run, it's a pleasant cruise past forest and field to the Winans Meadow trailhead at mile 1.6.

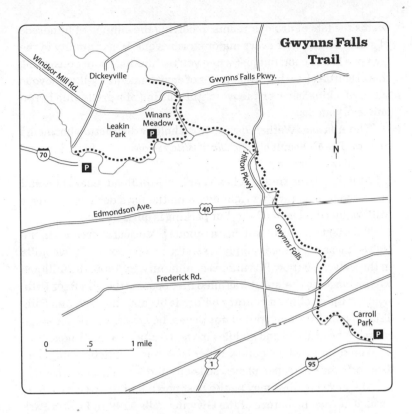

Gwynns Falls Trail

Windsor Mill Rd.

Dickeyville

Gwynns Falls Pkwy.

Winans Meadow

Leakin Park

Hilton Pkwy.

70

N

Edmondson Ave.

40

Gwynns Falls

Frederick Rd.

Carroll Park

0   .5   1 mile

1   95

Winans Meadow has ample parking, restrooms, and an infor-mation kiosk; for this reason, it is perhaps the more frequently used access point for the Gwynns Falls Trail. The path parallels Dead Run, an aptly named major tributary of the Gwynns Falls. Virtually the en-tire watershed of Dead Run is developed, with little surface area that is not paved or otherwise impervious to rainfall. Hence, even minor storms flash-flood the little stream with torrents of muddy, polluted water. Much of the riverbed has been scoured down to bedrock, and there is little aquatic life.

At mile 2.0, the trail crosses a pretty bridge spanning Dead Run and dumps onto Wetheredsville Road, permanently closed to ve-hicular traffic. Wetheredsville Road runs adjacent to the Gwynns Falls proper, a creek about thirty feet wide in winter and just a trickle during a summer drought. The river flows noisily over small rap-ids and would be a true delight except for the incredible amount of trash, especially plastic bags, that clings to riverside vegetation. Such seems the fate of urban streams, receiving the effluvia of hundreds of storm drains after every major storm event. Water quality in the Gwynns Fall is poor. But just when you're thinking about consigning this urban creek to the lower circles of environmental hell, the joyous rattle of a kingfisher or the watchful waiting of a great blue heron enlivens your day.

The area near Wetheredsville Road holds a distinction in cinema history. The 1999 cult classic *Blair Witch Project* was filmed in part in the adjacent forest.

At mile 2.7, the trail reaches Windsor Mill Road. Bear right and cross the bridge, turning right again on the far side. The Windsor Mill trailhead is located here, but parking is quite limited.

This next section of trail has a unique historical character. In the 1800s it was a millrace, supplying water and its power to five mills in the Calverton (now Rosemont) community. By 1900, the millrace was no longer in use, and it was filled in to become the Mill Race Path, popular for strolling a century before it became the Gwynns Falls Trail. This portion of trail is not paved, however. There are some rocks in the trail bed and puddles in wet weather, so road bikes, children on training wheels, and strollers will find it difficult going. The drop-off is quite steep in places, so keep children well supervised.

The next 1.5 miles may be the best portion of the Gwynns Falls Trail. The bucolic nature of the Gwynns Falls Trail in Leakin Park is unexpected, given its location well within the city limits. Much of the trail is quite isolated from the surrounding urban bustle, and the views are of a forested stream valley that could easily be mistaken for one in rural Baltimore County. There are surprisingly many wildflowers here, including spring beauty, jack-in-the-pulpit, violet, day lily, and jewelweed. Big old trees, especially oaks, tulip poplars, and American beeches, tower over the path, keeping it cool even in the hottest weather.

Paving resumes near Hilton Parkway, and the trail drops steeply off the hillside to floodplain level. After crossing several busy streets, the trail encircles Leon Day Park, named for the Hall of Fame baseball player and Baltimore native. This trailhead at Leon Day Park has parking and restrooms and is 3.0 miles from the Winans Meadow Trailhead.

In the next mile the trail passes through Western Cemetery, and there are splendid views of the river as it runs over the fall line. There are several large rapids at high water, including a dramatic eight-foot waterfall. Two busy road crossings bring you to Carroll Park, where there is ample parking just off I-95.

The trail continues eastward from Carroll Park, but the route is too convoluted to describe and is mostly on city streets. One fork leads to the Inner Harbor, while the other passes through Middle Branch Park. From here, there are superb views of the Baltimore skyline, as you look across the broad expanse of the tidal Patapsco River. Should you be truly interested in an urban hiking or cycling venture east of Carroll Park, you'll need to get the Gwynns Falls Trail map produced by the City of Baltimore.

Return on the same route, but don't miss a side trip that is not an official part of the Gwynns Falls Trail. At the intersection of Windsor Mill Road and Wetheredsville Road, continue on Wetheredsville Road as it parallels the Gwynns Falls in an upstream direction. A ride of 0.65 miles through a pretty forested landscape brings you to the historic mill community of Dickeyville. This is arguably Baltimore's most charming neighborhood, an isolated enclave of meticulously kept homes, many constructed from the native stone of the valley.

Once back at the Winans Meadow Trailhead, energetic cyclists may want to explore the many short foot trails that connect the highlights of Leakin Park: the Carrie Murray Outdoor Education Center, the historic Orianda House and even a miniature railroad (the Chesapeake and Allegheny Live Steamers), which operates one Sunday a month in pleasant weather. The trailhead at I-70 is another 1.6 uphill miles away.

Directions

From the Baltimore Beltway (I-695) take I-70 east; the sign is marked "local traffic only." Go to the end and park in the median between the eastbound and westbound lanes. To reach the Winans Meadow trailhead, take exit 14, Edmondson Avenue, east from the Baltimore Beltway (I-695). Go 1.9 miles. Turn left on Winans Way. Go 1.3 miles to the trailhead.

Cyclists arriving from Washington, DC, may find it more convenient to park at the Carroll Park trailhead, just off I-95. Take exit 51 off I-95. At the bottom of the ramp, turn left on Route 1, Washington Boulevard. Go 200 feet to the entrance to Carroll Park, on the left.

Other Outdoor Recreational Opportunities Nearby

Leakin Park is circumscribed by a four-mile hiking trail. The nearest state park, Patapsco Valley, is about a 20-minute drive away.

OSAGE ORANGES AND MASTODONS

Eastern North America was a much more exciting place in the late Pleistocene epoch, 13,000 years ago, than it is now. Large animals roamed the landscape, including mammoths, mastodons, saber-toothed tigers, and even 400-pound beavers. The fossil record shows that many of these species of "megafauna" went extinct about 12,000 years ago, at the end of the last Ice Age. Not coincidentally, humans arrived from East Asia about that same time, crossing over a land bridge between what is now Siberia and Alaska and then dispersing across much of North America in a surprisingly short period of about a thousand years. Paleontologists believe these new human residents hunted a majority of the large Pleistocene mammals to a rapid extinction.

Consider now the osage orange tree. Native to a small area in Oklahoma and Texas, osage orange trees were widely planted as "living fences"; their branches grow in a dense, unorganized filigree. Short, sturdy thorns help to keep cattle and other large animals at bay. An old saying was that an osage orange fencerow was "horse high, bull strong, and hog tight." Osage orange trees grow easily from rootstock, and so have been transplanted to every state in the lower forty-eight. Only a few dozen feet tall, they are unprepossessing trees, rarely noticed until autumn when their fruits develop.

Osage orange fruits are the size of softballs, greenish-yellow in color, with many convolutions and fissures in the outer surface. Kids often refer to them as "monkey brains," and the moniker seems appropriate. When cut open, the fruit exudes a sticky white sap and has a faint citrus-like odor (but is not related to oranges). Not every fruit has seeds, but those that do have many sunflower-sized seeds. What is most remarkable about the fruits and their seeds is that nothing eats them. No large or small mammals, no birds, no insects. Nothing.

This makes no sense. The purpose of a fruit, in evolutionary terms, is to entice an animal to eat it. The seeds then pass through the digestive tract of the animal and are eventually excreted. In this way, a stationary organism like a tree gets to spread its progeny randomly over the landscape, where some might survive and thrive in a new location. But if no animals eat the fruit or seeds of osage orange trees, why use energy to produce them?

What scientists have proposed is that osage orange fruits were eaten by one or more species of the now-extinct Pleistocene megafauna. These large herbivores, like mammoths and mastodons, then excreted the seeds, each with its own clump of fertilizer, in locations far from the parent tree.

It's an interesting hypothesis. It's logical, it takes several disparate facts and connects them in a sensible framework, and it explains a conundrum. The problem is that the hypothesis is not testable by experimentation and cannot be verified by observation. We may never know for certain if extinct mammoths and mastodons ate osage orange fruits, but it's an enticing mind picture and a challenging idea to contemplate.

Jones Falls Trail

Section: Cylburn Arboretum to the Baltimore Streetcar Museum
County: Baltimore City
Distance: 6.4 miles one way
Type: Multi-use recreational trail with some sidewalks and a few streets
Surface: Asphalt, concrete
Difficulty: Moderate. Some hills
Hazards: Traffic at road crossings and on a few short sections on streets, a few steep hills
Highlights: Urban forests, the Maryland Zoo, a sylvan dell, the Baltimore Streetcar Museum, Howard Peters Rawlings Conservatory and Botanic Gardens
More Information: https://jonesfallstrail.us
Street Address: 4915 Greenspring Avenue, Baltimore, Maryland 21209 (Cylburn trailhead)
GPS Coordinates: 39.350445, 76.659401 (entrance to Cylburn Arboretum)

Urban areas are known for their human diversity: diversity of races, cultures, lifestyles, and jobs. But urban landscapes are also quite diverse: neighborhoods where people live, parks where people recreate, and even forgotten places where almost no one goes. The Jones Falls Trail connects all three of these urban sites, and more. If you want to gain an appreciation for what Baltimore, or at least part of it, is like, cycle the Jones Falls Trail, located in the north-central section of the city. It's a surprisingly varied and unexpectedly pleasant recreational trail that begins in an upscale city community and ends in a remnant of Baltimore's industrial past, traversing a long-established municipal park along the way.

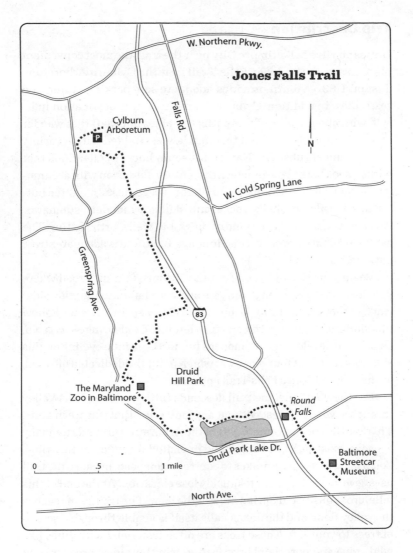

The Jones Falls Trail is 6.4 miles as described, one way. It is marked in two ways: with signage atop a six-foot pole and with a painted stencil on the trail surface, whether that surface is the dedicated off-road asphalt trail, concrete sidewalk, or paved street. Although the route is well marked, you must pay close attention to catch the unexpected turn or the occasional gap in signage at a critical place.

Trip Description

Unless you live in Baltimore City near the trail, the most convenient place to access the Jones Falls Trail is at the Cylburn Arboretum. Just off I-83, Cylburn provides adequate safe parking, water, and restrooms. In addition, Cylburn is an interesting destination in itself, with about a mile of footpaths (no bikes allowed) that wander among beds of flowers and through lawns studded with a variety of trees and shrubs. The Nature Museum houses collections that harken back to the late-nineteenth-century obsession with accumulating menageries of stuffed animals, bird eggs, nests, mounted butterflies, fossils, seashells, rocks, and skulls. By modern standards, it's an unusual and quirky kind of place, but well worth visiting. The gates to Cylburn are closed on Mondays, but there is adequate street parking just outside.

Begin your ride by cycling out the Cylburn entrance road where you drove in. Pass through the gate and turn left onto the wide sidewalk, without crossing to the far side of Greenspring Avenue. Follow this sidewalk for fifty yards, and turn left into Coldspring New Town, an upscale development of modern homes. Continue cycling on this sidewalk for about four blocks, at which point the dedicated off-road, asphalt-paved Jones Falls Trail appears.

For the next mile, the trail descends into the Jones Falls Valley through a wooded forest without any indication that you are in a city. This land has been a remote part of the Arboretum grounds for many decades, existing undisturbed and unvisited for much of that time. You'll need to use your brakes to control your speed, because the trail uses several switchbacks to quickly lose elevation. At the end of this mile, cross busy Cold Spring Lane at the light. The trail soon reaches the valley floor, and the Jones Falls itself is visible through a screen of trees to your left. Those trees are often festooned with vines like wild grape and porcelainberry, fast-growing botanical creepers and climbers that eventually will pull these trees crashing to earth. There are lots of multiflora rose, greenbrier, and spicebush that form a dense undergrowth, hosting familiar birds like cardinals and robins. This short section has the feel of one of those deserted corners of Baltimore where no one goes and which no one appreciates.

At mile 1.8, the trail emerges from nature into the quaint neighborhood of Woodberry, running along a lightly used city street lined with older houses constructed of the local Jones Falls stone. As the Woodberry light rail station comes into view, turn right on Clipper Park Road. Again, you are cycling on the road, sharing it with local traffic entering the trendy Clipper Mill area. It's a mix of new construction and beautifully rehabilitated old foundry buildings. Beginning in 1853 and for a century thereafter, the Poole and Hunt foundry was a mainstay of industry in Baltimore. It produced the iron brackets for the columns of the United States Capitol, and its pit lathe could turn out an iron wheel sixty feet in diameter. A fire in 1995 ended most industry here and provided an opportunity for perceptive developers to rebuild and rehab the stone shells of some of the remaining buildings.

Follow Clipper Park Road to Parkdale Road and turn left. Within 200 yards, the route enters Druid Hill Park and becomes an off-road recreational trail again. For the next half mile, the trail passes through a beautiful and lightly visited section of the park. Mature trees, many more than a century old, cast a deep shade; tulip poplar, American beech, and several species of oak dominate. The trail rises from the valley onto the uplands on a series of switchbacks. Trail advocates have planted a number of native and garden varieties of flowering plants along here, including Virginia bluebells, wild ginger, and columbine, creating a more interesting flora than the usual urban aliens and invasives. Once on the upland, watch for flying Frisbees; a portion of the park's disc golf course winds its way among the trees.

At mile 3.0 the trail emerges from the forest into a grassy meadow studded with the occasional specimen tree. It's a popular area for picnicking, and dogs and children cavort in a pastoral scene. To the left is a black fence marking the land set aside for the Maryland Zoo in Baltimore, and the formal entrance to the Zoo is found at mile 3.5. Another half mile of travel on path, sidewalk, and lightly traveled roadway brings you to the Rawlings Conservatory, one of the gems of Baltimore architecture and an underappreciated tourist destination. The centerpiece is the Palm House, a five-story greenhouse with walls and ceilings of glass housing towering old palm trees and related botanical wonders. In cold weather it's a warm and inviting stop on your bike ride, and in any season both the Palm House and the other three greenhouses are well worth a visit. The Conservatory is open Wednesday through Sunday, 10 a.m.–4 p.m.

Continue east on the Jones Falls Trail, riding about a quarter way round the large Druid Lake. Construction in this area, slated for 2017–22, may cause this portion of the Jones Falls Trail to be rerouted, so stay alert for signage. Near the tennis courts, follow the painted trail symbols on the wide sidewalk downhill to the park exit. Cross the Jones Falls on Wyman Park Drive; in some years, yellow-crowned night herons nest in the trees below the bridge and are closely visible from that vantage point. Immediately after crossing the bridge, the trail bears right down steep switchbacks to Falls Road. Lock your bike to the rack and walk down some decaying steps to a platform overlooking the Jones Falls.

Here is one of the most surprising and charming natural views within the Baltimore City limits. Set in a shady dell is Round Falls, a curving man-made dam with about a ten-foot vertical drop into a foamy pool. City noise is left behind, and there is a sense of serenity at Round Falls that belies its urban location and industrial past.

Round Falls

Returning to your bike, coast downhill on the sidewalk along Falls Road. The next three-quarters of a mile pass through a forgotten backwater of Baltimore, a relic of a time when the Jones Falls was the industrial heart of the city. The few remaining businesses are mostly warehouses and fenced parking lots. The Jones Falls itself burbles along adjacent to the trail, flowing over rocks and small rapids on its course to the Inner Harbor. Water quality is abysmal; the Jones Falls collects the effluent of the city's many chronically leaky sewer lines, and that aging infrastructure often endures acute major breaks as well. The entire west side of the stream is a forty-foot high wall of native stone constructed perhaps a century ago, built to tame the Jones Falls and consign it to the shallow valley. A few trees hang on in this dismal landscape, lending a scraggly shade in places. Just when you are ready to relegate the lower Jones Falls to environmental purgatory, a Paulownia tree's purple flowers lend a pleasant fragrance to the spring air, or a night heron stalks crayfish in the stream. The Jones Falls is always surprising.

At mile 6.4, the trail reaches the Baltimore Streetcar Museum, a nostalgic ode to the still-remembered days when public transportation in the city ran off overhead lines instead of on tires. It's not an upscale major tourist destination, and it's in a hard-to-reach forgotten corner of the city, but the Baltimore Streetcar Museum is worth a visit as you cycle the Jones Falls Trail. This point marks the end of the recreational trail portion of the Jones Falls Trail. Return to Cylburn by the same route.

Directions

From the Baltimore Beltway (I-695) take I-83, the Jones Falls Expressway, south. Take exit 10A, Northern Parkway, turning right. At the first stoplight, turn left on Greenspring Avenue. Go about 200 yards to the Cylburn Arboretum entrance.

Other Outdoor Recreational Opportunities Nearby

Lake Roland Park is located a few miles to the north; it has one nice walking trail. If you have your own canoe or kayak, it can be launched onto the lake.

WHITE-THROATED SPARROWS

"Oh sweet Canada, Canada, Canada" echoed through the March forest and was answered by several other such whistled songs. The singers were white-throated sparrows, a familiar bird at feeders and along brushy edges all winter long. By March, however, they are getting restless, singing persistently, almost ready to push north to their summer breeding grounds. Like the quack of a wood frog and the unexpected green of skunk cabbage leaves, the song of a white throat is a symbol of the imminent change in season.

Those who feed birds throughout the winter have no doubt seen white-throated sparrows often. Their bodies are small and stocky, with a dull brown plumage that is unremarkable. The feathers of the head are more colorful. In addition to the eponymous white throat, there is a bright yellow patch between and just above the bill and eye called the supraloral. Of more interest are the three cranial stripes: one on each side of the head, sometimes referred to as "eyebrows," and a median stripe atop the head, reminiscent of a Mohawk haircut. On about half the birds in any large group, these feathers are white; on the other half, tan. Either sex can have tan stripes or white stripes. A casual observer might suspect the tan-striped birds are a different species from the white-striped, or are at least evolving toward that end. Unfortunately, that casual observer would be wrong; the reality is far more interesting.

It turns out that a tan-striped bird will mate only with a white-striped bird; this rule applies to both sexes. Known as a disassortative mating system, the white stripe results from a genetic anomaly called a chromosomal inversion. (Chromosomes are how DNA, the genetic material in plants and animals, is packaged to fit into the nucleus of the cell.) A large segment of chromosome 2 somehow got turned around and then was reinserted backward into the location on the chromosome it had just left. Birds with the normal chromosome have tan stripes; birds with the inversion have white stripes. Since white is dominant over tan, 50 percent of all offspring will be white and 50 percent tan (on average), thus maintaining the feather polymorphism in the population.

But there are many other genes on this inverted chromosome, and one or more affect behavior. Scientists have observed that tan males invest heavily in parental care of the young and in guarding their mates from the attentions of other males, while white males spend much time advertising their presence by singing from a perch, intruding themselves into the territories of other mated pairs, and even sneaking in a surreptitious copulation with another male's female mate. Tan females also invest heavily in parental care of nestlings, while white females tend to be promiscuous. It's a classic case of a trade-off in reproductive strategy: will a white-throated sparrow leave more genes with the next generation by reproducing often with poor parental care, or by reproducing less often with good parental care? Of course, animals (and even humans) don't actually think about reproductive strategies, but our behavior indicates that we make such choices without conscious thought, and those choices are based in our genetic heritage. It's hard to believe that a common winter visitor to our bird feeder could provide us with a window into how we live.

Patapsco Valley State Park: Avalon/Glen Artney/ Orange Grove Area

Section: Avalon/Glen Artney/Orange Grove Area circuit
Counties: Howard, Baltimore
Distance: 5.2 miles as described; circuit ride
Type: Lightly traveled park road, multi-use recreational trail
Surface: Asphalt
Difficulty: Easy. Flat with one hill
Hazards: None
Highlights: River valley, historic footbridge, cascade
More Information: Patapsco Valley State Park, http://dnr.maryland.gov
/publiclands/Pages/central/patapsco.aspx, (410) 461-5005
Street Address: 5254 South Street, Halethorpe, Maryland 21227
(park entrance)
GPS Coordinates: 39.219932, 76.705009 (park entrance); 39.227595,
76.725300 (Avalon trailhead)

Patapsco Valley State Park is another of Maryland's linear greenways, flanking both sides of the Patapsco River from where it flows, tiny and narrow, through the rich farmland of Carroll County to tidewater in the industrial backyards of Baltimore. It is known locally as the "River of History": Lafayette's soldiers camped along its shores on their way to join Washington's forces at Yorktown; Benjamin Banneker, our country's first black man of science, lived and died near the Patapsco; and the valley was the site of the first commercial railroad line in the United States. Located within easy reach of millions of Marylanders, "Patapsico" (as the locals pronounce it)

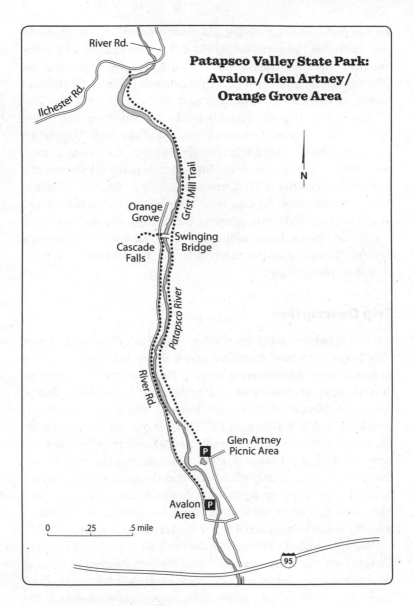

Patapsco Valley State Park:
Avalon/Glen Artney/
Orange Grove Area

River Rd.

Ilchester Rd.

N

Grist Mill Trail

Orange
Grove

Swinging
Bridge

Cascade
Falls

Patapsco River

River Rd.

Glen Artney
Picnic Area

P

Avalon
Area

P

0   .25   .5 mile

95

is one of the state's most familiar parks. The land preserved by Patapsco Valley State Park is frequently quiet, always beautiful, and well worth a visit.

The Avalon/Glen Artney/Orange Grove section of the park is a scenic and pleasant site for a bike ride. It is often shady and cool, even in midsummer, with big, old trees overhanging the road and trail. In winter, the north-facing River Road lies entirely within the shadow of the steep hillsides and will not see sunlight for months. Wildflowers abound, especially in spring and fall, and the riparian habitat makes birding a rewarding pastime.

The bicycle trip described here is a 5.2-mile loop ride in the Avalon/Glen Artney/Orange Grove area of the park. The circuit was made possible only fairly recently (1992) by the paving of what was once a muddy service road. This 2.3-mile portion, known as the Grist Mill Recreational Trail, was specifically designed to be accessible to the disabled. An eight-foot-wide blacktop lane is bordered by a three-foot-wide strip of gravel, providing a contrast in texture underfoot. Sturdy metal railings line the trail wherever there is a dropoff. The rest of the ride is on roads open to park traffic, but vehicle use is typically light.

Trip Description

Enter this portion of Patapsco Valley State Park from Route 1 near Halethorpe, Maryland. An entrance fee is charged at a contact station a short distance after entering the park. Pass under the Thomas Viaduct, the first multiple-stone-arch bridge built in the United States; more than 150 years after its construction, it still carries a major railroad line south to Washington, DC. This is ironic, because on the day the bridge first opened to rail traffic in 1835, everyone but the engineer who designed it believed it would collapse into the river. Follow the road to a T junction, turn left to cross the river, and park in the large lot near the picnic pavilions at Avalon. Wheelchair-accessible bathrooms and water are available here, except in very cold winter weather. Athletic fields and a playground are located nearby.

Begin your ride by re-crossing the Patapsco River into Baltimore County over the bridge on which you drove in. Instead of turning right toward the contact station, continue straight for 50 yards and then turn left. Within a quarter mile, this narrow road ends at the Glen Artney area and Lost Lake. An artificial pond rebuilt after the ravages of Hurricane Agnes in 1972, Lost Lake is popular with fishermen, especially after early spring stockings. Several mulberry trees line the upland edge of the parking lot, and their fruiting in late spring attracts many songbirds.

The far end of the Lost Lake parking lot marks the start of the Grist Mill Trail. Enter the trail, located on a narrow bench of land bordered by the railroad and a seasonally flooded wooded wetland. Spring peepers and American toads are the most common amphibians in this swamp, using the puddles for vernal breeding. This is good birding habitat as well, especially in early morning; you may want to walk the obscure footpaths that wind through here to the riverbank for the best chance of seeing pileated woodpeckers, warblers, ospreys, and ducks.

The trail continues upstream, although it is separated from views of the river in most places. The alluvial floodplain, scoured in 1972, still has some big trees, but it is dominated by a dense tangle of spicebush, box elder, and small maples. In winter, the southern exposure keeps this part of the trail pleasantly warm and sunny, in contrast to the icebound River Road on the shaded opposite bank of the Patapsco.

After a little more than a mile, the paved trail reaches the ruins of the Orange Grove Flour Mill, built in 1856 and destroyed by fire in 1905. Only a few foundation walls are left of the six-story building in which flour was ground using dammed-up river water to power three large millstones. This mill was reputedly the largest flour mill east of the Mississippi River; its premier brand was "Patapsco Superlative."

Continue cycling upstream through a shady forest with fine views of the river. Another half mile brings you to the site of Bloede Dam, undergoing deconstruction and removal as of this writing (2017). Built in 1906 to supply electricity, this was America's first hydroelectric dam where the turbines were placed below the spillway. The dam only produced power until 1924; thereafter it became a safety hazard, as kids slid off the 27-foot-high face of the dam into the recirculating waters below. In the decade prior to dam removal, six people died here.

The trail ends at Ilchester Road. Return to the site of the flour mill and cross the Patapsco River on the Swinging Bridge, a landmark familiar to generations of Marylanders. For more than a century, kids have visited this bridge in its various incarnations. This flat, open area is known as Orange Grove (named after the osage orange trees that grew here long ago). Once the site of eight mill workers' houses, it is now a parking lot and has a water fountain and wheelchair-accessible bathrooms.

A short hike originating from Orange Grove is well worthwhile. Park and lock your bike in the rack provided and walk about 200 yards up the blue-blazed Cascade Trail, the entrance to which is located between the comfort station and the large parking lot. The trail is steep at first but then flattens out and becomes merely rocky. After about 150 yards, the trail reaches an enchanting little dell overhung with hemlocks and witch hazel. An eight-foot-high waterfall, Cascade Falls, tumbles over a rocky ledge into a clear, frigid pool and makes a pleasant picnic spot on a hot day. The surrounding forest hosts a diverse selection of native wildflowers, especially in spring, including bloodroot, spring beauty, wild ginger, and jack-in-the-pulpit. Most visitors retrace their steps to the parking lot, but some continue onward, connecting with the steeper and more difficult upland trail system of the park. If you're interested in this sort of hiking, obtain a map of the area's trails online from the Maryland Department of Natural Resources.

Returning to your bike, leave the parking area, heading downstream on River Road. It is usually open to vehicular traffic but is rarely busy; nevertheless, watch for cars, especially if you have small children with you. Pedal up a hill (the only one on this circuit) for a nice view of the valley. The road continues on, bordered by steep, heavily forested hillsides occasionally split by sparkling creeks in steep ravines. Displays of spring wildflowers are excellent all along here, and in autumn the foliage is beautiful.

About a mile downstream of Orange Grove, the road emerges from the forest at a rocky outcrop to give a good view of the valley and Lost Lake. Note how the far shore of the Patapsco has been reinforced with baskets (called gabions) containing large rocks to ensure that floodwaters do not erode the berm separating Lost Lake from the river. Coast down the hill to your car at the Avalon parking lot, completing a 5.2-mile circuit.

Directions

From the Capital Beltway (I-495) take I-95 north to I-195, the exit for BWI airport. From the Baltimore Beltway (I-695) take I-95 south one exit to I-195. Follow the I-195 exit east, toward BWI airport. At the first exit off I-195, turn south on Route 1. As the exit ramp dumps you onto Route 1, go only 50 yards and turn right on South Street. The entrance to Patapsco Valley State Park, called River Road, is on your left.

REMOVING A HISTORIC DAM

With a roar that shook the ground and sent a shower of concrete, gravel, and dirt across the river valley, Bloede Dam was breached by explosives on a September day in 2018. Work began soon after on the aged dam's removal. More than a century old, Bloede had long altered the ecology of the Patapsco River, and had also been a significant public safety hazard. Its demolition marked a new era for the river, one characterized by a more natural gradient, improved water chemistry, a more diverse riparian biota, and greater resiliency against the insults of development and human activity upstream.

Today, there is no longer any trace of Bloede Dam save an informational panel on the adjacent Grist Mill Trail in Patapsco Valley State Park. The river now dances and sparkles over dark boulders of the local gabbro rock, free after having been tamed under a sediment-filled reservoir for the past century. Steep, eroded riverbanks have been graded into a more natural slope, and stabilized by native grasses, shrubs, and trees. Sunlight fills the valley, and birdsong enlivens the air. What was once an industrial, human-centric working river is now a place of pastoral serenity.

Bloede Dam had an interesting history. Constructed in 1906, it was the nation's first dam to generate power using turbines placed inside the dam. The electricity it produced supplied the nearby communities of Ellicott City and Catonsville. Within a few years, however, the dam was decommissioned as cheaper sources of electricity became available, and the generators were shut down after just seventeen years of operation. The dam was sold to the State of Maryland in 1938, and was a thorn in the side of park staff ever after. A few times each year, kids would get injured sliding down the sloping dam face, and at least nine deaths have been reported since 1980.

(continued)

Dams like Bloede block passage of migratory fish like shad, herring, alewives, and eels, cutting them off from their native spawning grounds. The original design of the dam included a wooden fish ladder. In 1992, the State constructed a concrete fish ladder on one side of the dam, at a cost of $1.58 million. Both were ineffective. Removal of the dam opened up more than 60 miles of river and tributaries suitable for use by spawning anadromous fish. While shad and river herring numbers have increased only modestly since then, eel numbers have exploded, from just 53 in 2019 to more than 37,000 (estimated) in 2022. While eels may not be a very charismatic fish, they do play an important role in river ecology. For example, Eastern elliptio mussels require eels to complete their life cycle. The most common mussel species in Maryland, the elliptio improves water quality by removing algae, excess nutrients, and even harmful chemicals. Mussel larvae hitch a ride upriver by attaching to the gills of American eels, thus dispersing throughout the watershed.

Nationwide, more than 1,000 dams have been removed since 1990, and on average about 50 more are taken down each year. Even so, less than one percent of dams nationwide are being considered for removal. Many still serve a useful purpose; hydro-power is a cheap and clean energy source. All dams, however, have major effects on the ecology of their rivers. Expect to see more dams taken down in future years, but many decisions to do so will be controversial.

Northern Central
Railroad Trail

Section: Ashland to the Pennsylvania border
County: Baltimore
Distance: 19.7 miles one way
Type: Multi-use recreational trail
Surface: Crushed limestone
Difficulty: Easy. Flat, with some slight steady uphill gradient
Hazards: A few road crossings
Highlights: River valley, rolling farmlands
More Information: Gunpowder Falls State Park, http://dnr.maryland.gov
/publiclands/Pages/central/gunpowder.aspx
Street Address: Not available
GPS Coordinates: 39.501309, 76.633835 (Paper Mill Road); 39.579262,
76.615422 (Monkton Station)

O f all the good ideas that have ever been proposed to benefit the
public, one of the best has been the conversion of abandoned
railroad rights-of-way into recreational trails. Such linear greenways are often among the few remaining tracts of land available for
purchase in suburban regions and connect population centers with
more sparsely settled rural areas. They provide corridors for wildlife, too, and often are surprisingly natural in setting. Rail trails have
proven immensely popular with almost everyone. The Northern
Central Railroad Trail (NCRT) is nationally famous, and may well
be the best of its kind

The NCRT extends due northward from the suburbs of Baltimore for 19.7 miles. Originating at Ashland, the trail follows the Gunpowder River, Little Falls, and then Bee Tree Run upstream to the

Pennsylvania border. In 2007, the NCRT was formally renamed the Torrey C. Brown Rail Trail, in honor of Dr Brown, past Secretary of the Maryland Department of Natural Resources and an ardent trail advocate. However, the name most commonly used in conversation is still the "NCR Trail. Beyond the Mason-Dixon line, the trail is called the Heritage Rail Trail and extends 21 miles to York, Pennsylvania. The Maryland portion of the NCR Trail is administered by Gunpowder Falls State Park.

Since its opening in 1984, the NCR Trail has been one of the most popular outdoor recreational facilities in Maryland. Walkers, joggers, cyclists, cross-country skiers, birdwatchers, fishermen, tubers, and equestrians all flock to this unique resource. Although it's not a place to find solitude, the linear nature of the trail ensures you of some space of your own. Nature lovers will find an unexpected diversity of plants and animals, owing in large part to the adjacent river corridor.

The trail itself is a generous 11 feet wide in most places, ample space for a biker to pass a strolling couple. It is composed of a type of crushed rock that is about the consistency of heavy sand and makes a firm surface for biking. The trail drains well, even after a heavy rain, and most puddles will have disappeared within 24 hours. The NCR Trail has no hills, but its northern half rises steadily in elevation. It is a great place for even the youngest riders, as well as strollers and wheelchairs. Access is generally good, although parking lots and road crossings near Baltimore are often full on weekends. Park somewhere north of Monkton and you'll be rewarded with fewer trail users.

Trip Description

You may begin your ride on the NCR Trail at any of the road crossings, but only two have enough parking to accommodate a large number of cars. If you arrive late on a pleasant weekend day, plan on parking along Paper Mill Road near the southern terminus of the trail, or at Monkton, near the halfway point. Paper Mill Road has a parking lot and extensive shoulders for additional parking but no other facilities. In contrast, Monkton has bathrooms, water, trash cans, a few picnic tables, a ranger station (open only on weekends), and a store that sells snacks (again open only on weekends). Because

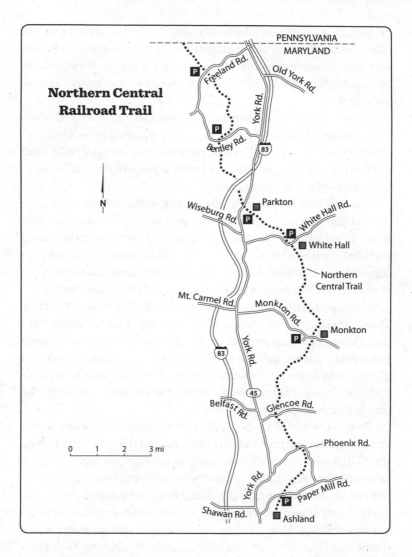

Northern Central
Railroad Trail

PENNSYLVANIA
MARYLAND

Freeland Rd.
Old York Rd.
York Rd.
83
Bentley Rd.

N

Wiseburg Rd.
Parkton
White Hall Rd.
White Hall
Northern
Central Trail

Mt. Carmel Rd.
Monkton Rd.
Monkton
83
York Rd.
45
Belfast Rd.
Glencoe Rd.
Phoenix Rd.

0 1 2 3 mi

York Rd.
Paper Mill Rd.
Shawan Rd.
Ashland

most cyclists approach the trail from the south, the ride is described from south to north.

The NCR Trail originates in Ashland, an old mill community that time and development seemed to have forgotten—until the 1980s. The old mill houses have now been rehabilitated and sell for a price previous tenants would have thought a king's ransom. New townhouses have sprung up, and suburbanites barbecue on decks overlooking the trail's origin. Fortunately, creeping upscale development is left behind after the first few hun... other side of the trail are the upper reaches of Loch ... implementation has created extensive marshes common reed; red-winged blackbirds and great blue he... quently seen.

Shortly the trail crosses Paper Mill Road, the busiest ... road crossings. Use particular caution here and walk your ... intersection. Fortunately, at this point the worst of the NC... lies behind you, and you can look forward to more pastoral sc... between here and Pennsylvania.

The trail now becomes mostly shaded, with medium-sized ... overhanging the path. In some places, private property reaches to t... edge of the trail and a scattering of houses lie adjacent to it, most... from the era when the railroad connected outlying towns with the commerce of Baltimore. These dwellings are never intrusive, however, and the older houses lend a rustic simplicity to the scene.

The sound of flowing water is never far away from the NCR Trail. The southernmost half borders Big Gunpowder Falls, a narrow river that alternately sparkles over rocky riffles and flows through deep green pools. Water quality is excellent; indeed, a resident population of trout lives in the cool, shaded waters. There are occasional floodplains with beautiful stands of summer wildflowers, although the trail is always at a higher elevation.

To build this level roadway the railroad made liberal use of cuts and fills. Today, only the cuts are obvious, and there are many along the NCR Trail. Here, rock outcroppings are exposed, and their dark color and the deep shade contribute to a sense of foreboding as the path winds between rock walls. Many ferns poke out of crevices or spray across slopes where soil has accumulated, and their appearance is striking. Most are hay-scented ferns, but cinnamon and Christmas ferns are common, and a few royal and New York ferns may be found. Curiously, in many of the northern cuts pure stands of ferns are sheltered exclusively by red maple. A sunny fall afternoon makes these places vibrant with rich colors.

Perhaps the most scenic section of the trail is that between the junction of Little Falls with the Gunpowder River and the tiny community of Parkton, between miles 9 and 13. Little Falls is a lively small stream here, flowing noisily over large boulders and through waterworn chutes. The sound of water music and the close proximity of the trail are most pleasant and invite tired cyclists to rest in the cool shade and dip hot, tired feet into the soothing waters.

Another interesting area lies between miles 17 and 18, south of Freeland. Here, a beautiful little wetland is situated adjacent to the west side of the trail. Unlike river floodplains, a wetland such as this one has a constant high water table throughout the year. Standing water is found here; it is sometimes obvious and sometimes not, lurking under hammocks of vegetation where an unwary step can result in a wet, muddy foot. These nontidal wetlands are fairly common along the Maryland-Pennsylvania border and harbor their own unique flora and fauna. Red maples and alders dominate the shrub layer, while water-loving species like cinnamon fern, sensitive fern, skunk cabbage, steeplebush, and Joe-Pye weed are found covering the mud. Many kinds of bacteria and algae grow on and in the mud. Oxygen penetrates poorly into this substrate, resulting in the "rotten-egg" odor of hydrogen sulfide being given off when the mud is disturbed. These wetlands have a distinctive appearance to even the casual observer because of their unusual flora. More reclusive is the fauna of these wetlands, the most interesting member of which may be the bog turtle. These small turtles, identified by a slash of color along the side of the head, remain buried in the weeds of nontidal wetlands and are almost impossible to find.

This northern section of the trail rises almost imperceptibly uphill, but walkers or cyclists will not get winded. Because the change is gradual, you may not notice it as you pedal northward. The return trip for the most northerly three miles, however, takes about half as much time as the outbound trip.

The Pennsylvania line is reached without fanfare and is marked only by a gate. Turn your bike around and note that, wherever you started from, you're now halfway home. But the downhill nature of the trail makes for smooth sailing, and the return trip is always faster. The Northern Central Railroad Trail is the finest bike path in Maryland; would that we had more recreational trails like it.

Directions

The Northern Central Railroad Trail approximately parallels I-83 north of Baltimore, and the latter road provides easy access. From the Baltimore Beltway (I-695) take I-83 north. To reach Paper Mill

Road, take the Shawan Road exit east from I-83. Go 0.8 mile and turn right on York Road, Route 45. Proceed 0.3 mile and turn left on Ashland Road. This soon becomes Paper Mill Road; continue until you cross the NCR Trail and park along the road shoulder or in the lot.

To reach Monkton, take I-83 north to the Mt. Carmel Road exit. Go right (east) for 0.5 mile, and turn right on York Road, Route 45. Proceed only about 200 yards and then turn left on the obscurely marked Monkton Road, Route 138. Cross the river, continue for 0.2 mile, and park in the lot next to the old train station. In the event that this lot is full, return the way you came, cross to the west side of the river, and make an immediate left onto Old Monkton Road, where there is roadside parking.

Other Outdoor Recreational Opportunities Nearby

The Big Gunpowder River downstream of Monkton is excellent for canoeing and kayaking, at least when a suitable amount of water is being released from Prettyboy Dam, located upstream. Floating the river in inner tubes is also a popular activity in summer, especially in the vicinity of Monkton; on hot days expect to encounter tubers hiking the NCR Trail, tube over shoulder, as they walk to the starting point of their float. There are many good hiking trails in the nearby Gunpowder Falls State Park.

BOG TURTLES

Few animals in Maryland are as obscure in the public mind as the bog turtle. Confined to a series of wet meadows along the Pennsylvania border in Carroll, Cecil, Baltimore, and Harford Counties, bog turtles occupy a habitat where we humans rarely venture. Even if you decide to wade into the mixture of mud, water, dense vegetation, and insects that forms these nontidal wetlands, you're unlikely to come across a specimen of *Clemmys muhlenbergii*. Scientists working with the species say that locating a bog turtle requires almost a sixth sense—a feeling that one clump of grass looks "turtley" while the next one over does not.

Bog turtles are North America's smallest turtle (three to five inches in length), brown, and inconspicuous. They are easily identified by a yellow, orange, or reddish blotch on each side of the head. Like most turtles, they are omnivorous, eating insects, some plant material, and carrion. Bog turtles move around very little; radio-tagged turtles are frequently found within a few yards of their previous location. In part, this sedentary nature may be due to the limited size of their habitat, since most of the Maryland bogs and wet meadows in which they are found are quite small. Sexual maturity is reached after five to eight years. Mating occurs in the spring, and nesting may be delayed for several months. Females dig a rough depression in elevated ground, especially mossy or grassy tussocks. Three to five eggs are typically laid, and these hatch in early September. Bog turtles may live for twenty to thirty years in the wild if undisturbed.

Maryland is at the southern edge of the distribution of bog turtles but harbors as many as one-third of the worldwide population. Because of this small population size, limited distribution, unusual habitat requirements, and the species' popularity with reptile collectors, Maryland listed the bog turtle as a threatened species in 1976. That action stimulated research on bog turtles, and they were subsequently found at over 170 sites in the Free State. Since the bog turtle is now a state and federally protected species, the greatest threat to these turtles in Maryland is habitat loss; farmers and developers may drain wet meadows or change the drainage pattern that supplies water to the wetland. In addition, encroachment by woody vegetation can negatively affect bog turtles; grazing by cows and goats can help maintain the grasses and sedges bog turtles need. Controlled burns of the habitat in winter when the turtles are hibernating in burrows is also useful in killing woody vegetation. Finally, known bog turtle habitat is sometimes purchased from willing sellers by the Department of Natural Resources, as occurred in 2014. These steps, together with strong nontidal wetlands legislation, will ensure the continued existence of this harmless and obscure reptile.

Chesapeake and Ohio Canal Towpath

Section: Section 1: Great Falls Tavern (mile 14.4) to trail's origin in
   Washington, DC (mile 0)

   Section 2: Harpers Ferry area: Brunswick, Maryland (mile 55.0)
   to Shepherdstown, West Virginia (mile 72.8)

   Section 3: Paw Paw Tunnel area: Route 51 (mile 156.2) to Little Orleans,
   Maryland (mile 140.9)

   Section 4: Cycling the entire length of the towpath (mile 0.0 to mile 184.5)

Counties: Section 1: Washington, DC, Montgomery

   Section 2: Frederick, Washington

   Section 3: Allegany

   Section 4: Washington, DC, Montgomery, Frederick, Washington, Allegany

Distance: Section 1: 14.4 miles one way

   Section 2: 17.8 miles one way

   Section 3: 15.3 miles one way

   Section 4: 184.5 miles one way

Type: All sections: Multi-use recreational trail

Surface: Gravel and dirt, with some mud in wet weather

Difficulty: Easy. No hills; seemingly flat but with a slight uphill (east to west)
   grade

Hazards: Crowds in Section 1

Highlights: Maryland's longest trail; scenic river valley; history; nature

More Information: C&O Canal National Historical Park, (301) 739-4200;
   www.nps .gov/choh

Street Address: Section 1: 11719 MacArthur Boulevard, Potomac,
   Maryland 20854 (Great Falls Tavern)

   Section 2: 100 South Maple Avenue, Brunswick, Maryland 21716
   (MARC train parking lot)

   Section 3: no address available

GPS Coordinates: Section 1: 39.000253, 77.248145 (Great Falls Tavern)
  Section 2: 39.311595, 77627729 (MARC train parking lot)
  Section 3: 39.544140, 77.461521 (Paw Paw Tunnel parking lot)

The longest trail in Maryland, the C&O Canal towpath, is admirably suited for leisurely strolling, active day hiking, overnight backpacking, and bicycling. Cyclists may choose a variety of day trips, or opt for multiday rides, either camping at hiker/biker sites along the towpath or finding overnight accommodations at trailside motels or inns along the way. In this chapter, I suggest three different one-day rides that include some of the most beautiful scenery and interesting terrain found along the 184.5-mile towpath. In section 4, I provide logistical information for cyclists who wish to ride the entire towpath in three, four, or five consecutive days of pedaling.

Before setting out to cycle the C&O Canal towpath, there are a few things you should know in advance.

First, the trail is 184.5 miles long, and each mile is denoted by a stone or wooden marker about two feet high, with the mile number (from the origin in Washington, DC) inscribed. Keep alert for these mileposts in order to gauge your progress.

Second, the surface is gravel and dirt, with some muddy spots in wet weather. The "gravel" usually consists of pulverized local stone, which often includes slate, and slate has sharp edges. Flat tires are far more common on the towpath than on other nonpaved, multiuse recreational trails in Maryland, many of which are composed of crushed limestone, a far more benign surface. Be sure to carry a flat tire kit containing the necessary tools, and have the knowledge and experience needed to patch and change a tube. I also recommend carrying a spare, never-used tube, especially for multi-day rides. I do not recommend skinny-tired road bikes for riding the towpath. Don't forget a small pump that will fit into your pack.

Third, the towpath often has a distinguishable uphill and downhill to it. It may appear flat to the eye, but cycling west (upstream) is usually more difficult than riding in the easterly direction. Furthermore, because the surface is gravel and dirt, even the dead flat portions slow your maximum speed by several miles per hour in comparison to what you could do on crushed limestone paths. You'll find that there are few opportunities to coast on the towpath.

Fourth, get into shape for cycling before embarking on a multi-day ride, or even a long one-day ride, on the towpath. The rough surface generates more bumps than your average trail, so your butt needs to be well conditioned. Similarly, a mile on the towpath requires more caloric output than a mile on an asphalt trail. These two factors mean that whatever mileage you can easily cycle on an asphalt trail should be cut by about one-third on the towpath. Don't bite off more than you can chew—this is supposed to be fun.

Fifth, obey all National Park Service rules. Do not exceed 15 miles per hour. Pack out all your trash. Alert hikers as you come up on them with a verbal or bell warning. Yield to horses and mules. Ride single file and stay to the right. Walk bikes over aqueducts.

Because the scale of a map spanning 184 miles would be too small in this format, I refer you to the National Park Service website (https://www.nps.gov/choh/planyourvisit/maps.htm) for more useful detail.

Trip Description

Section 1: Great Falls Tavern (mile 14.4) to trail's origin in Washington, DC (mile 0)

This section of the C&O Canal towpath is by far the most crowded. You are likely to encounter people walking, strolling, hiking, and cycling at all hours of the day and even the night. If you are looking for a ride exclusively for the purpose of exercise, there are better places to cycle. However, if you enjoy history, scenery, people, and occasional breaks off the bike to explore your surroundings, this easternmost portion of the towpath is a fine choice.

I have chosen to describe this trip from west to east, from Great Falls Tavern (mile 14.4) to the trail's origin in Washington, DC. Unless you live in the District, parking is far more available and traffic easier to deal with when you start outside the Washington Beltway (I-495).

Great Falls Tavern houses a National Park Service Visitor Center, and its parking lot has space for several hundred cars. Nevertheless, on pleasant weekend days between mid-April and mid-October, there is often a line of vehicles waiting for someone to leave. Arrive before 10 a.m. or after 4 p.m. to better your chances of finding a spot at such times. There are restrooms and drinking water available here year-round, and a snack bar that is sometimes open during the warmer months. The Tavern itself has some interesting displays of canal history, and staff can usually answer questions about the canal, towpath, and trail conditions.

From the parking lot, cross the re-watered canal in front of the tavern on a small footbridge and turn left on the towpath. You'll often find it difficult to ride here due to the crowds, but a rewarding footpath to spectacular views of Great Falls is only a quarter mile away, so you can easily walk your bike to this point (mile 14.1). Since bikes are prohibited on this side trail, lock your bike securely before walking the boardwalk to the falls overlook.

Cross the footbridge to Olmstead Island. This footbridge was washed away during Hurricane Agnes in 1972 and rebuilt twenty years later. Olmstead Island and the adjacent Falls Island are covered by a bedrock terrace forest that is one of Maryland's most unusual and rare natural features. Scoured by episodic floods, the only plants to survive are hardy, fast-growing trees and shrubs and herbaceous plants that have found a foothold in pockets of undisturbed alluvial soil. Virginia pine, post oak, and red oak dominate the drier soils on the islands, while pin oak, river birch, and swamp white oak are found in depressions with poor drainage where the soil is often wet. These islands are home to some of the rarest and most unusual herbaceous plants in Maryland, including McDowell's sunflower, wild false indigo, and hairy wild petunia. More than 300 kinds of plants and animals here are tracked by the Maryland Department of Natural Resources as "species of concern." Please stay on the boardwalk so as to avoid damage to the vegetation.

Within a few hundred yards, the boardwalk ends at the Great Falls overlook, surely one of the most spectacular viewpoints in the entire National Park system. Here, the Potomac drops more than 75 feet over the hard, erosion-resistant rocks of the Piedmont, creating a cascade of tumbling and roaring whitewater. At high flows, the ground shakes underfoot with the power of the river. At low flows, expert kayakers navigate the chutes and falls on a regular basis, usually early in the morning before the crowds arrive. It is humbling to realize that several times in the past century, major floods have covered everything you can see, even the rock underfoot, with immense volumes of brown, churning floodwaters.

Return to the towpath and mount your bike; more natural wonders await in the next mile. Within 200 yards there are dramatic views into the Mather Gorge below Great Falls. A bit farther east is a

sign indicating the entrance to the Billy Goat Trail (mile 13.8), arguably the most scenic and challenging hike in Maryland. Energetic
cyclists may want to consider a stop to hike this trail, but it will take
several hours; if you plan to ride all the way to the towpath's origin
and back, it will be a long and tiring (but rewarding) day outdoors.

The next 1.5 miles eastward contain a variety of habitats crammed
into a small area that should not be missed by anyone interested in
nature. That said, the towpath has been washed out near mile 12.7,
and cyclists will have to carry their bikes while hopping from rock to
rock for about a dozen yards. There is a well-marked bicycle detour
for the less agile called the Berma Road, but take it only if you must;
the next mile of towpath is just too interesting to miss.

Along this stretch of towpath is Widewater, a natural pond incorporated into the canal that is popular with fishermen. Vernal pools
dot the landscape where rainwater has accumulated atop the impervious rock of Bear Island; these miniature ponds abound with
mating wood frogs in March, spring peepers and American toads in
April, and other amphibians in May and June. Places where drainage occurs have dry soils where you'll find fence lizards, red cedar
trees, the grasses broomsedge and little bluestem, and the spring
wildflowers bluets and moss phlox. There are superb displays of
ephemeral wildflowers in late April, including bloodroot, columbine,
spring beauty, squirrel corn, sessile trillium, toothwort, and golden
ragwort, to name just a few; this area may have more kinds of spring
wildflowers than anywhere else in Maryland. But the crowning glory
of the spring wildflower season here are the acres of rich alluvial soil
packed with Virginia bluebells, their pendulous blue flowers tinted
the same hue as the summer sky. Late April and early May bring a
wide variety of migrating songbirds who use the Potomac as a corridor leading west to the mountain ridges; among the species elusive
or uncommon elsewhere but seen or heard regularly here are prairie
and worm-eating warblers and yellow-billed cuckoos. A cyclist with
an interest in nature will find it hard to cover this mile in any less
than three hours.

Another major towpath access point is at the Old Angler's Inn
parking lot (mile 12.3), usually filled to capacity all day in the summer and on weekends. Eastward from here, the crowds diminish so
that riding is a less congested endeavor. Between mile 9.5 and 7.3,
seven locks raise the canal 56 feet in elevation, and this is a chance to

marvel at the stonework involved. Near mile 3.5, an iron truss bridge appears over the canal; it carries the Capital Crescent Trail, a paved multi-use trail that now runs adjacent to the towpath for the next 2.5 miles eastward. It's a good alternative for your return trip, as it is more shaded than the towpath, a salutary feature in hot weather.

At mile 3.2 is Fletcher's Boathouse, a fine place to take a break. There are shady mature trees, picnic tables, bottled water and snacks for sale, and canoe, kayak, and rowboat rentals. The remaining miles into Georgetown (a colonial village now incorporated into Washington, DC) are notable for their urban character. The church spires of Georgetown tower above the towpath, but the walls of nearby buildings hem in the narrow trail. It crosses several city streets at grade, where care should be exercised. Canal boat rides are popular with tourists here; what that means for cyclists is that you should watch out for mule "scat" on the towpath, and if you encounter mules, you should dismount and let them pass. Finally, the trail emerges onto a shady lawn that marks the towpath's origin. Note that at this point the towpath intersects the Rock Creek Trail. Reverse your route to return to your car.

Cyclists will want to understand that the wide sidewalks near the beginning of the C&O Canal towpath in Washington, DC, form a hub that opens up a variety of off-road (except for busy intersections), multi-use trails. From the origin of the C&O Canal towpath, you can turn left on the Rock Creek Trail, cycling to the National Zoo and parts of Rock Creek Park. On weekends, you can continue north through the Park on car-free Beach Drive to the northern section of the Rock Creek Trail. From where the trail leaves the District, it continues for 12 miles to Lake Needwood. Alternatively, you can leave the Rock Creek Trail at its intersection with the Capital Crescent Trail and take that trail west and south for about 7 miles to its intersection with the C&O Canal towpath, making a 22.5-mile circuit. In the other direction, from mile zero of the towpath, take the wide sidewalks (bicycles allowed) due south to Thompson's Boathouse, then bear left along the Potomac for about a mile to the vicinity of the Lincoln Memorial. From here, you can ride the paths of the National Mall, or continue south on lightly used roads through Hains Point Park, or cross the Potomac on the Arlington Memorial Bridge. Once in Virginia, you can ride the Mount Vernon Trail both upstream and downstream for many miles.

Section 2: Harpers Ferry Area: Brunswick (mile 55) to Shepherdstown (mile 72.8)

This section of the C&O Canal towpath has both beautiful scenery and dramatic history, each of which alone would qualify it for inclusion in this book. In the area around Harpers Ferry, the Potomac River has cut its way through the Blue Ridge, and the surrounding hills are more than a thousand feet higher in elevation than the river and town. Additionally, the fabled Shenandoah River unites its waters with the Potomac at this point. In terms of history, two signal events occurred in Harpers Ferry. In 1859, John Brown and a few followers took over the US Armory in the town, hoping to incite an anti-slavery rebellion. It was quickly quashed, and John Brown was hung for his actions, but the event is widely credited by historians as contributing to the start of the Civil War just eighteen months later. In September 1862, Confederate troops under General Thomas J. "Stonewall" Jackson forced the surrender of more than 12,000 Union soldiers who were surrounded in the town. The event remains the largest surrender of US soldiers in our nation's history.

Start your ride from the MARC train lot in Brunswick, Maryland, located off South Maple Avenue between the westbound and eastbound tracks. The towpath may be accessed by riding toward the river, crossing the eastbound tracks with care. Turn right, west.

For most of the next three miles, the towpath and canal are separated from the Potomac River by several dozen yards of riparian forest, so there are rarely water views. Even so, the path is enjoyable; large sycamores and silver maples shade the trail, and a variety of wildflowers edge the towpath. Use care; stinging nettles are common, as is poison ivy. Be aware that the latter grows as both a three-leaved woody plant about a foot in height and as a hairy vine climbing many feet up tree trunks. The towpath is wide enough that these vegetable nasties are easily avoided as long as you stay out of the weeds.

The C&O Canal here is a wet ditch filled with small trees, shrubs, wetland plants, and fallen tree limbs. There's not enough water to float a canoe, but neither is there so little that the canal can be crossed dryshod. In spring, frogs, toads, and salamanders lay eggs in the water, and their mating calls can be cacophonous. Mosquitoes and "river gnats" can be problematic at certain times of the year, but cyclists are only bothered when they stop.

At mile 58, the famous Appalachian Trail joins the towpath. Southbound hikers on the AT have just descended Weverton Cliffs, 500 feet of steep elevation change located just north of the towpath; they will share the trail with you for the next 3.7 miles. And a wonderful stretch this is. The towpath soon runs closer to the Potomac, revealing beautiful views of both the river and the surrounding mountains. The Potomac is studded with rocks, and some significant rapids with names like White Horse, Maui Wave, and Mad Dog are within easy view of the cyclist. The surrounding mountains rise more than a thousand feet above the river. Three states are in view: Maryland, where you are cycling; Virginia, on the far side of the river;

and West Virginia, where the little town of Harpers Ferry occupies the triangle of hilly land between the Potomac and Shenandoah Rivers. To paraphrase Thomas Jefferson, the view is worth crossing the ocean to see.

What makes this cycling trip unique is the opportunity to explore the historic town of Harpers Ferry. To get there, follow the well-marked signs at mile 60.7. You can lock your bike to a rack along the towpath or carry it up a circular wrought iron staircase to the pedestrian bridge over the Potomac. Walk the bike over the bridge and lock it to the rack in town. Either way, the views from the pedestrian bridge are astounding. The black cliffs of Maryland Heights rise from the Free State side of the river; vultures often soar on the thermals created by these palisades. The red brick buildings and church spires of Harpers Ferry rise stepwise up the West Virginia hills, while Short Hill in Virginia is just imposing in its bulk. The two rivers, Shenandoah and Potomac, meld their waters below; in warm weather tubers drift in the lazy currents of the Potomac, while whitewater rafters float by on the Shenandoah, enjoying a respite after the Staircase rapids.

On the far side of the footbridge is a small park containing several interpretive signs; few places in America have so much history and natural beauty crammed into such a small space. Ahead and to the left is a replica of the Fire Engine house, which John Brown and his followers occupied after raiding the Armory. Civilians and local militia quickly laid siege to the Fire Engine house. The next day, a small contingent of United States Marines stormed the building, killed several of the raiders, and captured the rest, including John Brown.

Shenandoah Street is about three blocks long and is managed by the National Park Service. The buildings have all been restored to their mid-nineteenth-century appearance and house museums and displays. There is a bookstore and gift shop, and restrooms and drinking water are available. Potomac Street, perpendicular to Shenandoah Street, also has many restored buildings, but most house shops and restaurants. Walking uphill, be sure to hike to Jefferson Rock for views of the surrounding water gap. The campus of Storer College, a historically black institution now owned by the National Park Service, is nearby, as is the Appalachian Trail Conservancy office and visitor center. Taken together, it's easy to spend several hours exploring Harpers Ferry.

Returning with your bike to the C&O Canal towpath, continue riding west, upstream relative to the river's flow. Within 200 yards, a footbridge crosses the canal, leading to a hiking trail to the top of Maryland Heights (and beyond). This diversion from cycling is also worthwhile, if you have the time and energy. On the opposite side of the towpath, the Potomac flows busily over small rapids and rock shelves in a section known to paddlers as the Needles. At summer low water, this area is popular with folks of all ages riding inner tubes down the river; there are several commercial outfitters that supply gear and shuttles.

At mile 62.3, an old dam, now mostly broken out, spans the river. Above this point, the river is flat and calm, and the towpath is a pastoral place. The big trees host Baltimore orioles in late spring and early summer; indeed the entire length of the C&O Canal is prime nesting habitat for our state bird. Since they mostly occupy the treetops, the best way to find orioles is to be familiar with their song.

Antietam Creek aqueduct, mile 69.4, is perhaps the best preserved of the stone bridges that carry the canal and towpath overtop of streams that flow into the Potomac. Completed in 1834, it spans the small river that gave its name to the major Civil War battle. Antietam National Battlefield is itself worth a visit, and a cycling tour of its roads and key features is described elsewhere in this book. Note that although the battlefield is only about two miles from the towpath, there are some steep hills and roads without shoulders in between.

Mile 72.7, where Route 34 crosses the river, canal, and towpath on a high bridge, marks the terminus of this ride. A lovely old brick house and its attendant agricultural fields here are beautiful on summer mornings as the mist rises and dissolves in the sunlight. Route 34 leads into Shepherdstown, West Virginia, a charming village with many nineteenth century houses. On the river, rocky bluffs mark the point where, in 1787, James Rumsey demonstrated the first steamboat, two decades before the more famous Robert Fulton did so. Derided as "a canoe powered by a teakettle," the boat achieved a top speed of four miles per hour.

This point marks almost 18 scenic miles of cycling on the towpath; return by the same route to Brunswick for a total distance of 35.6 miles. Should you anticipate that this distance will be too much, turn around short of Shepherdstown; just remember that whatever point you turn around at is halfway and plan accordingly.

Section 3: Paw Paw Tunnel Area (mile 156.2) to Little Orleans (mile 140.9)

This is the westernmost of the three single-day recommended rides on the C&O Canal towpath in this book. While most of the towpath is pastoral, many of the 15.2 miles of this trip traverse a mountainous region of Maryland that is quite remote. The trip also includes riding through the 3,118-foot-long Paw Paw Tunnel; from the middle, each end is little more than a pinpoint of light, and it's hard to see your hand in front of your face. Finally, there's a visit to a classic country store, a unique slice of Americana.

Begin your ride from the C&O Canal National Historical Park access and campground where Route 51 crosses the Potomac River. There is parking here for several dozen cars, vault toilets, well water pumped by hand, and more than a dozen campsites. The campsites (tents only) are primarily used by paddlers starting their Paw Paw Bends trip from this point. The towpath is at the back end of the parking lot. Turn right and pedal a half mile to the tunnel.

The rest of the canal and towpath follow the Potomac River, but here engineers saw the chance to shorten the route by six miles by tunneling through the mountain. It proved a disastrous choice. A project that was expected to be completed in two years actually took almost fourteen and brought the owners to the edge of bankruptcy twice. Construction began in 1836, from both ends simultaneously. It was crude work: black powder was used to blast the rock into rubble, men cleared the debris with pick and shovel, and mules and carts then hauled the rock out. Progress was slow; ten to twelve feet per week was typical. Working conditions were harsh, the location was remote, and most of the immigrant workers were unskilled and untrained. The initial crew of Irish immigrants was upset when English, and then German, workers were hired. There were strikes in 1837, 1838, and 1839, involving both physical violence and destruction of property. Cholera took some workers, who were buried at Purslane Cemetery, just off the towpath at mile157.4. The canal company ran out of money in 1842, and no construction was done from then until 1847. The Paw Paw Tunnel opened to boat traffic in 1850 and operated until 1924.

The National Park Service recommends you dismount and walk your bike though the tunnel. The walkway is not wide, perhaps five or six feet. The packed clay and soil underfoot has potholes, some filled with water, and muddy spots. A flashlight or bicycle headlamp is recommended, although you should certainly turn off all lights near the halfway point to experience the near-total darkness of the tunnel. There is a simple but sturdy fence between the walkway and the canal a dozen feet below; some of the rails are original, polished and bearing grooves worn by towropes over the decades. Almost six million bricks line the tunnel.

The towpath emerges from the tunnel in a deep chasm hollowed from the surrounding shale. Some interesting plants grow from cracks in the rock, including butter-n-eggs, coral bells, columbine, common mullein, and asters. The wet soil of the old canal supports jewelweed, Joe-Pye weed, cardinal flower, and cattails.

Remounting your bike, continue pedaling in a downstream direction. Pass Sorrel Ridge hiker/biker campsite, popular with canoe and kayak campers who, having paddled seven miles from their Paw Paw launch site, find themselves only a mile's walk by towpath from their car. Handy when you leave some vital piece of camping gear in your vehicle.

The remaining miles to Little Orleans are quite scenic, with the placid river on one side and the hills of Green Ridge State Forest on the other. There is a dirt road near the towpath between miles 147 and 151, but it is a long way from anywhere and is lightly used. The only other signs of civilization are the three railroad trestles that cross the Potomac; the sound of a lonesome whistle and the clack of the rails is a part of every hike, ride, or paddle in Paw Paw Bends country.

This ride, as recommended, concludes at the Fifteen Mile Creek aqueduct, mile 140.9. It is one of the few places where a paved road reaches the river and has long been an outpost of civilization (of sorts). George Washington passed by here in 1784, and there has been a store at this site for close to 200 years. Long known as "Bill's Place," this old country store was legendary for its character when Bill Schoenadel and his wife owned it in the 1970s, 1980s, and 1990s. It's a combination saloon, convenience store, video arcade, bait shop, canoe livery, and restaurant. Until it burned in 2000, a weather-beaten and flybitten moosehead stared down from the wall at bar patrons, and more than 4,500 self-autographed one dollar bills were tacked to the ceiling. Locals were fond of saying that if you couldn't find it at Bill's, you didn't need it. The replacement building lacks the atmosphere of the original Bill's, but it's still worth a visit.

After fortifying your body, mind, and spirit at Bill's, it's time to return to your vehicle at Paw Paw. Should you decide to begin a hiking, cycling, or paddling trip at Little Orleans, make sure you don't park too close to the river; I've heard of Paw Paw Bends paddlers who arrive here after two rainy days on the river to find their car windows deep in muddy river water. Round trip, Paw Paw to Little Orleans is 30.6 miles.

Section 4: Cycling the Entire Length of the Towpath, 184.5 miles

Cycling the C&O Canal towpath is one of the great long-distance, off-road bike rides in America. At 184.5 miles in length, it takes most cyclists three or more days to complete. One managing agency, the National Park Service, provides information, patrols the towpath, and maintains the trail surface. Much of the distance has beautiful views, ranging from the pastoral to the wild. Virtually the entire trail is wooded, providing shade in summer. History, it seems, is always at hand for those who want to learn more about the past. There are ample accommodations in the form of inns, bed and breakfasts, and motels, spaced at comfortable intervals. The towpath also offers campsites, typically every five to seven miles, for those who prefer not to "taint their wilderness experience" with a soft bed. Bike-friendly public transportation links the two termini of the towpath, easing the logistics of a multi-day ride. Finally, and not least, 2013 marked the completion of another off-road, multi-use trail, the Great Allegheny Passage, that links seamlessly with the C&O Canal towpath. Together, these two trails stretch 335 miles, from Washington, DC, to Pittsburgh, Pennsylvania, making what some call "the ride of a lifetime." Indeed, cyclists from all over the nation flock to the GAP / C&O each year.

For a cyclist contemplating a multi-day ride on either or both of these trails, an invaluable reference is the *TrailGuide*, published annually by the Allegheny Trail Alliance (www.GAPTrail.org). It provides basic information about the trail experience, including mileages, elevation changes, and history. The C&O Canal towpath is treated as an equal partner with the GAP Trail (despite the name of the organization). More importantly, the *TrailGuide* also provides information (in the form of advertisements) for cyclist-friendly overnight accommodations and places to snack, dine, and resupply.

Transportation logistics. The simplest way to get to the start and home from the end of your ride is to have a friend drop you off and pick you up. Count yourself lucky if you have such saintly friends. Most cyclists, however, are left to their own devices for transportation.

If you have two cars, both capable of carrying bikes, gear, and people, it's possible to set up a shuttle for your trip. For example, drive to Washington, DC, park one car, and then drive to Cumberland with bikes, gear, and riders, where you will begin your ride. This is, of course, time-consuming; depending on where you live, you'll waste at least a half day on both ends of your trip just doing the shuttle. Long-term parking in Cumberland is available for a fee near the train station on West Harrison Street, within a stone's throw of the western terminus of the C&O Canal towpath. It's a wise idea to check in with the local police to alert them that your car will be staying overnight for one or more days. Long-term parking near the towpath's origin in Washington, DC, is problematical; downtown garages are expensive. One practical solution is to park at Ronald Reagan Washington International Airport's long-term parking lot (about $10 a day). The airport is only five miles from the terminus of the towpath, all of it on bike-friendly, wide sidewalks or dedicated paved, multi-use trails.

If all this sounds difficult and confusing, despair not. There is another option. Amtrak connects Washington, DC, Harpers Ferry (West Virginia), Cumberland (Maryland), and Pittsburgh (Pennsylvania) with their *Capitol Limited* train service. Since 2015, Amtrak has provided some trains with a baggage car equipped with bike racks, and for an extra $20 beyond the cost of your passenger ticket you can bring your bike. A few caveats are worth knowing, however. There are only eight racks per train, so reserve your ticket well in advance during prime cycling season. Tandems, recumbents, and trailers are not allowed because of their size. Remove your panniers as well, and either check them as baggage or keep them with you at your seat. In Washington, DC, the *Capitol Limited* departs from Union Station, five miles from the origin of the towpath via the Mall on wide sidewalks where bicycles are permitted. In Cumberland, the Amtrak station is just a few blocks west of the towpath's terminus. Cyclists living in or near Baltimore now have the option of taking bikes on weekend MARC trains connecting Baltimore-Washington International Airport with Union Station.

Accommodations logistics. Note that lodging is limited on the western third of the trail, between Hancock (mile 124) and Cumberland (mile 184.5). Your only option is a small and basic inn at Little Orleans (mile 141). Overnight accommodations are also quite limited on the eastern third of the trail, between Brunswick (mile 55) and Washington, DC. The C&O Canal Trust rents five different historic lockkeeper's houses for overnight stays in this section, at miles 5.4, 8.8, 19.6, 30.9, and 48.9. Only the two closest to Washington, DC, have running water and electricity; the others are extraordinarily rustic but constitute a unique and interesting experience. Reservations are required well in advance, since the houses are serviced by volunteers with the nonprofit organization.

For a three-day, two-night ride (about 62 miles per day), stay in Hancock, Maryland (mile 124), and Harpers Ferry, West Virginia (near mile 61). Both towns have many options for both dining and lodging.

For a four-day, three-night option (about 46 miles per day), stay in Little Orleans (mile 141), Williamsport (mile 100), and Brunswick (mile 55), all in Maryland. Accommodations in all three towns exist but are limited.

For a five-day, four-night option (about 37 miles per day), stay in Little Orleans (mile 141), Williamsport (mile 100), Harpers Ferry, West Virginia (near mile 61), and Leesburg, Virginia (near mile 36).

Food logistics. Better restaurants are found in Harpers Ferry, West Virginia, Hancock, Maryland, Cumberland, Maryland, and Washington, DC. There are also good restaurants in Leesburg, Virginia, and Shepherdstown, West Virginia, but a visit to either town requires a road ride with traffic since both towns are a few miles from the C&O Canal towpath. Convenience stores or very basic restaurants may be found in Leesburg, Brunswick, Harpers Ferry, Shepherdstown, Williamsport, Hancock, Little Orleans, Paw Paw, and Cumberland.

Water. Drinking water is available for purchase at convenience stores in the towns listed above. Although the National Park Service has water pumps at most (but not all) of the hiker/biker campsites, which are spaced roughly every 5–7 miles, that water is sometimes unpalatable. The water comes from a well, and to ensure its safety, iodine is added episodically. You'll want to drink such water only as a last resort.

Bike repair. As of this writing (2017), bike shops with repair capability are found in Leesburg, Brunswick, Shepherdstown, Hancock, and Cumberland.

Bicycle camping. The C&O Canal towpath is quite accommodating for those who prefer to camp rather than stay overnight in a motel or inn. For the most part, hiker/biker campsites are spaced about every 5–7 miles along the towpath. The exception is at the eastern end, outside of Washington, DC; the first campsite is at Swains Lock, mile 16.7. Each campsite has space for at least several tents, a fire ring, a portable toilet, and many have a water pump. (Call the National Park Service to check on water availability.) Some campsites have picnic tables. Virtually all have a view of the river, and only a few can be accessed by motor vehicle. (Any site near a road is invariably noisier and contains trash.) The National Park Service manages these hiker/biker campsites, which are first-come, first-served. They are shared with backpackers and paddlers doing multi-day trips. If you decide to camp on your towpath ride, you should probably reduce your daily mileage; your bike will be heavier and harder to pedal, and setting up and breaking down camp will take extra time.

If you plan to camp while cycling the towpath, it would be wise to invest in panniers or a trailer. Carrying a backpack with twenty or more pounds while cycling raises the center of gravity significantly and makes the cyclist unstable. Also, the lighter your load, the more comfortable your ride will be. Become familiar with the gear and mindset of "ultralight backpacking." Assuming your finances can handle it, invest in some new high-quality, lightweight gear; your two-person tent should weigh less than 4 pounds, your sleeping bag less than 2.5 pounds, and your sleeping pad less than 1.5 pounds. Overall, there's no reason you need to carry more than 20 pounds of camping gear, personal items, and food.

Directions

Section 1

To reach Great Falls Tavern from either Baltimore or Washington, DC, take the DC Beltway (I-495) west. The last exit in Maryland before crossing the Potomac River into Virginia is exit 41, marked

Carderock / Great Falls. Take it and proceed 1.75 miles west on the Clara Barton Parkway to its end. Turn left onto MacArthur Boulevard. Go 3.5 miles to the entrance to Great Falls Park.

Section 2

To reach Brunswick, Maryland, from either Baltimore or Washington, DC, take I-70 west. Just beyond Frederick, Maryland, take Route 340 west. Exit onto Route 180 toward Petersville. Go 1.7 miles and turn left onto Route 79, Petersville Road. Go 2.7 miles into Brunswick, and continue on Petersville Road through the traffic circle. Go right on South Maple Street to the MARC train parking lot.

Section 3

To reach the Paw Paw tunnel parking area off Route 51, take I-70 west from Baltimore or Washington, DC. Just past Hancock, exit onto Route 522 south. Cross the Potomac River into West Virginia. Go 5.5 miles. In the town of Berkeley Springs, turn right onto Route 9. Wind your way over the ridges for 22 miles. Just past the town of Paw Paw, West Virginia, cross the Potomac River into Maryland. Go 100 yards and turn right into the C&O Canal National Historical Park parking lot.

Section 4

To reach the western terminus of the C&O Canal towpath, take I-70 west. Just beyond Hancock, exit onto I-68 west. In Cumberland, take exit 43C. At the stoplight, turn left onto Harrison Street. Parking is available nearby. To reach the towpath's terminus, walk under the interstate. There is a National Park Service Visitor Center here.

The eastern terminus of the C&O Canal towpath is poorly accessible due to heavy traffic and little parking in downtown Washington, DC. For reference, it is a few yards away from the Rock Creek Parkway exit onto Pennsylvania Avenue. You may be able to find short-term parking (to drop off cyclists only) at Thompson's Boat Center. To reach Thompson's from the aforementioned intersection, continue south on the Rock Creek Parkway for perhaps 200 yards, then turn right on Virginia Avenue into the Boat Center.

SPRINGTIME EPHEMERAL
WOODLAND WILDFLOWERS

Among the most eagerly awaited and avidly enjoyed phenomena of the natural year in Maryland is the appearance of wildflowers each April on the forest floor. Confined to mature woodlands with rich, well-developed soils, a number of native plant species sprout, flower, set seed, and die back in the short space of two months or so. These ephemeral harbingers of spring share some common life history characteristics that link them to the ecology of their habitat.

The most common springtime ephemeral wildflowers in Maryland are trout lily, spring beauty, Dutchman's Breeches, rue anemone, and Virginia bluebells. Some other species that flower at the same time and in the same habitat but whose leaves persist for a longer period of time include bloodroot, mayapple, hepatica, and several species of trillium. All are perennial; most of the year is spent as a quiescent rootstalk.

All of these plants flower, but most do not release a large number of seeds. In fact, a flower like trout lily may put out fewer than ten viable seeds each year. In contrast, many annuals re-lease thousands or tens of thousands of seeds. In large measure, this is because annuals live in a variable, uncertain environment where the best strategy for success over time is to spread lots of progeny over lots of space in the hope that a few will survive. Conversely, in a stable habitat like a mature forest, conditions are suitable and unchanging over time, so the best strategy is to devote most energy and resources to vegetative growth of the perennial rhizome. Only a few seeds are produced, mostly as a counterbalance against the possibility of a disturbance to the habitat.

For this reason, springtime ephemeral wildflowers often spread asexually. Trout lily rootstalks (known as corms) will put out a long shoot called a "dropper" that penetrates the soil for several inches. The end of the dropper forms a bulbous swelling that later develops into a new corm and can be the source of

(continued)

new roots and shoots. Thus, a colony of these plants may actually be genetically identical individuals linked by a network of underground roots and droppers. This life history strategy often explains why such plants are frequently found in clusters.

Woodland wildflowers play an essential role in forest ecology. Pollen and nectar associated with flowers act as an important food source for a number of insects, especially bees and ants, at a time early in the season when other food sources are scarce. Springtime ephemerals also play an important role in the cycling of nutrients, especially the element phosphorus. Early spring rains dissolve nutrients in the forest floor litter and carry them downward through the soil, where they will eventually become less available to plants for growth. These vernal wildflowers, growing rapidly at a time when other plant life is still dormant, rescue nutrients for their own development. As they die back in late spring through summer, the released nutrients become available to other plants.

Another springtime ephemeral woodland plant is lesser celandine, which grows as a mat of bright green shiny leaves and has many yellow, buttercup-like flowers. This plant is not native and is highly invasive. Within living memory, lesser celandine has eliminated many kinds of native wildflowers on and adjacent to alluvial floodplains. In some areas, virtually no other herbaceous plant grows on the forest floor. Lesser celandine is almost impossible to eradicate; even white-tailed deer refuse to eat it. Unfortunately, lesser celandine can be expected to replace native wildflowers into the future. Their only redeeming (if it can be called that) characteristic is that they are ephemeral, the leaves completely dying back and disappearing sometime in May.

Antietam National Battlefield

Section: Battlefield circuit

County: Washington

Distance: 8.3 miles as described; circuit ride

Type: Mostly lightly traveled park roads; a short section on public roads

Surface: Asphalt

Difficulty: Moderate to strenuous. Hilly

Hazards: Traffic, especially in Sharpsburg

Highlights: Rolling farmland, battlefield site

More Information: Antietam National Battlefield, https://nps.gov/anti, (301) 432-5124

Street Address: 5831 Dunker Church Road, Sharpsburg, Maryland 21782 (visitor center)

GPS Coordinates: 39.474243, 77.744526 (Visitor Center)

Nestled in the rich farmlands of central Maryland, out where life is quiet and peaceful, lies the site of the most violent day in American history. Antietam National Battlefield exists today much as it did in September 1862. Corn ripens slowly in the summer sun; leaves wither, yellow, and drift sparsely down from autumn-tinged trees. Over one hundred and fifty years after fate brought together opposing armies, pastoral scenes still surround the battlefield, and the nearby town of Sharpsburg drowses quietly. No fast food restaurants, no wax museums, no motels blight Antietam, unlike so many of our other Civil War battlefields. It is a national treasure not just for what went on here long ago but for what it is today.

The Union Army of the Potomac attacked the Confederate Army of Northern Virginia here on September 17, 1862. Fighting was desperate, fierce, and bloody, sweeping back and forth across a relatively small piece of landscape. As the sun went down, casualties totaled 23,110 men. Exhausted, the two armies glowered at each other the next day before General Robert E. Lee retreated into Virginia. The battle gave President Abraham Lincoln the opportunity to issue the Emancipation Proclamation, freeing all slaves in the rebel states.

The field at Antietam is a fine one for bicycle touring. Of all the major Civil War battlefields, this is the least developed, so it is perhaps not surprising that visitation is light. Although cyclists share roads with auto tourists, the speed limit of 25 mph and the lack of crowds make pedaling the narrow, intimate roads a joy. The landscape is quite rough, with many rock outcrops, and there are a number of steep but short hills. Bicycling at Antietam is best for adults and older children who are experienced and have the necessary stamina. The loop described here is 8.3 miles in length.

Trip Description

Begin your bicycle tour at the National Park Service Visitor Center just off Route 65 north of Sharpsburg. Water, bathrooms, and information are available here. The Visitor Center has a small museum, a film presentation, and a Civil War bookstore. A fee is collected here for your use of the park.

Mount your bike and pedal in a northward direction, toward the clearly visible Dunker Church. Just 0.1 mile north of the visitor center, the Dunker Church is a plain stone edifice that marks the high ground on the battlefield. As such, it was the focus of repeated attacks by Union troops in the early morning hours of September 17.

Continuing north, the road passes through and eventually encircles the North Woods and the Cornfield. Monuments abound in this area, as so many men of both sides fought and died over these few acres.

At mile 2.0, the designated auto tour bears right onto Cornfield Avenue; instead, continue straight on the Smoketown Road. After 0.2 mile, turn left toward Mumma's Farm. At mile 2.8, turn left on Richardson Avenue. Paralleling this park road is an old sunken road known in military annals as the Bloody Lane. This salient in the Confederate defenses was the focus of over four hours of intense fighting

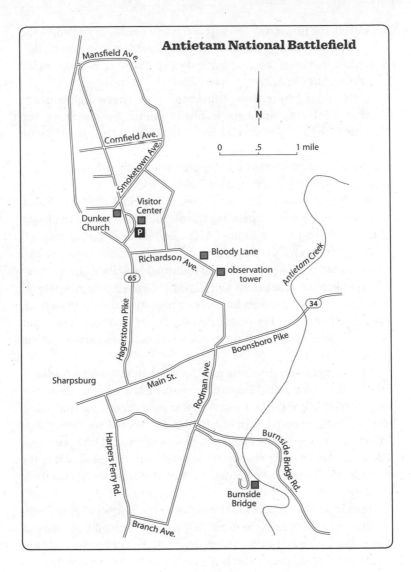

around midday on September 17. An observation tower at mile 3.1 provides a panoramic view of this portion of the field.

From the tower, the hilly, rural nature of the Antietam landscape is evident. There are a large number of rock outcrops poking through the earth in agricultural fields, and many fencelots are so rocky as to be suitable only for pasturage. The area around Antietam is underlain by limestone, a hard but erodable rock. In places where cracks or faults in the limestone develop, soil water can slowly dissolve the rock. Sinkholes, caves, and small but steep undulations in the terrain can result; this karst topography, as geologists call it, is best typified in Maryland by the Antietam area.

Soils derived from these limestone strata have high concentrations of calcium carbonate, leached from the rock by rainwater. Calcium carbonate acts as a buffer and maintains the soil pH in the neutral to slightly alkaline range. Such soils allow plants to take up nutrients more easily than many other soil types; thus such land is especially rich and valuable as farmland.

South of the observation tower, the road passes through an area that saw little fighting, separating the northern and southern phases of the battlefield. Cross Route 34, the Boonsboro Pike, at mile 3.8 and continue south for 0.6 mile to a T intersection. Turn left and take the road downhill for 0.4 mile to Burnside Bridge, the most famous landmark on the battlefield. Here 400 Georgia riflemen held off thousands of Union troops for hours, preventing these forces from cutting off Lee's line of retreat across the Potomac. This is a pleasant area for a picnic, and a 1.8-mile foot trail leads downstream along Antietam Creek.

Return uphill on the same road, cutting across the top of the T intersection, now called Branch Avenue. This area was the site of the final fighting of the battle of Antietam, occurring late in the day. Having finally crossed Burnside Bridge and routed the Georgians, Union troops were ready to fall on Lee's flank and cut off his escape. The Confederate Army was saved by the timely arrival of A. P. Hill's division, which had just completed a forced march of 17 miles from Harpers Ferry.

At mile 6.3 of this bike tour, turn right onto Harpers Ferry Road, a public road with no shoulders. However, the speed limit here is still only 25 mph and traffic is not heavy. As you enter Sharpsburg, turn right on Main Street, Route 34, being careful of traffic. After one block, turn left on Route 65, South Church Street, also known as the Hagerstown Pike. As this is the main intersection in town, it might be prudent to walk bikes across it. Route 65 is less heavily traveled and has good shoulders; it will return you to the visitor center at mile 8.3. Should you desire not to ride on public roads, it would be possible to retrace your route from Burnside Bridge, thus ensuring that all travel is within the national battlefield.

The Sunken Road (Bloody Lane)

Much of the Antietam battlefield is prime habitat for bluebirds. These beautiful but shy birds prefer open, agricultural land bordered by hedgerows with tree cavities for nesting. Since bluebirds will also use artificial nesting boxes, the Park Service has placed a large number of them on fenceposts around the battlefield. Look for a flash of blue and an undulating flight pattern as you ride.

Directions

From Washington, DC, or Baltimore take I-70 west. Exit south onto Route 65 and proceed about nine miles. The visitor center is just off the main road and is well marked by signs.

Other Outdoor Recreational Opportunities Nearby

The National Park Service maintains a walking trail through the Antietam battlefield that is distinct from the paved roads. Ask for a map at the Visitor Center. In addition, the C&O Canal towpath is only a few miles away, and it is very beautiful and peaceful in this area. Antietam Creek is a pleasant, easy canoe trip as well, when it has sufficient water (typically in winter and spring, and within 48 hours of a hard rain in summer and fall).

BLUEBIRDS

Few birds in the eastern United States are more beloved than bluebirds. Fabled in song and folklore, they are a companionable species that adapts fairly well to human activity. Shy and unaggressive, bluebirds appeal to both the eye and the ear. In the last forty years or so, bluebirds have made a comeback, due in large measure to human intervention. Their conservation is a good example of how successful the science of wildlife management can be.

Bluebirds are unmistakable denizens of farms, fields, and open country. Just a bit larger than a sparrow, males are bright blue on the back with a rusty chest; females are somewhat duller all over. In Maryland, many birds overwinter in small flocks, occupying areas with sufficient winter food supplies (mostly berries and other fruits). By March, the birds spread over the landscape, investigating nesting cavities in trees, fenceposts, or bluebird boxes. Eventually, a male will set up a territory around a suitable cavity and defend it against all comers while trying to attract a female. If he is successful, the female will build a cup-shaped nest of rootlets, weed stems, grass, and small twigs. After mating, the female usually lays four or five pale blue eggs and incubates them for about two weeks. The blind, helpless chicks develop rapidly and leave the nest after another two weeks. The male bluebird will often tend these fledglings for several more weeks as they learn to gather their own food (now mostly insects). Meanwhile, the female may lay another clutch of eggs; no sooner is the first brood independent than the process begins again for the exhausted parents. Juveniles of the first brood frequently help feed subsequent broods, an altruistic behavior that is not common among bird species. In some cases, a third clutch may occur, so that family duties extend well into August.

A little-known fact about bluebird mating habits is that monogamy is not always the rule, despite the appearance of domestic bliss in bluebird families. In one study, up to 25 percent of broods were fathered by more than one male. Either sex may be polygamous if given the opportunity.

By 1970, bluebirds were a declining species in Maryland and in most of their breeding range throughout the eastern United States; one estimate was that populations had declined by 90 percent in the twentieth century. Bluebirds were no doubt affected by the use of pesticides in the period between 1945 and 1972. However, the single most significant factor was loss of suitable nesting cavities. There were two causes. First, widespread use of metal fenceposts, more intensive management of woodlots that included removal of dead trees, and loss of hedgerows and edges from agricultural lands all decreased the number of available nest sites. Second, house sparrows and starlings, both alien species that expanded their range over this same period aggressively competed with bluebirds for the nesting cavities that were left. Starlings are larger birds, and they will almost always displace bluebirds. House sparrows are a more even match, but aggressive individuals sometimes kill bluebirds, usually pecking through the front of the skull.

Fortunately, we humans have helped by saturating the landscape with bluebird houses and increasing the public's awareness of the plight of bluebirds. The species readily accepts these boxes, and it is thought that about 90 percent of all bluebirds nest in these artificial cavities. It is probably impossible to have too many bluebirds, however, given the enjoyment they impart to us. So lend a hand by setting out bluebird houses in areas of suitable habitat.

Western Maryland Rail Trail

Section: Big Pool to Pearre
County: Washington
Distance: 23 miles one way
Type: Multi-use recreational trail
Surface: Asphalt
Difficulty: Easy. Eastern half is flat; western half has a slight uphill grade
Hazards: A few road crossings, some steep drop-offs at trail's edge protected only by plastic fencing
Highlights: Floodplain forest, shale and limestone cliffs
More information: Fort Frederick State Park, dnr.maryland.gov/publiclands /Pages/western/fortfrederick.aspx, (301) 842-2155
Street Address: Near 11124 Big Pool Road, Big Pool, Maryland 21711 (near Big Pool trailhead)
GPS Coordinates: 39.624035, 78.017054 (Big Pool trailhead)

The century from about 1850 to 1950 was the heyday of the railroad. In many ways, railroads opened up the western United States to settlement, connecting California, Oregon, and Washington to the other contiguous states. East of the Mississippi, rail lines reached into almost every town and village. In Maryland, places that are now isolated rural hamlets, or even remote river valleys and mountaintops, were once served by locomotive and freight car. Laid out on a map, railroad lines look like nothing so much as the arterioles and capillaries of the human vascular system that reach every part of the body.

The Western Maryland Railroad was an important rail line in the state of Maryland, connecting Baltimore City with the coal fields of

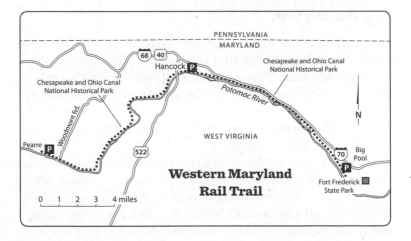

West Virginia and Pennsylvania via a route that followed the Potomac River west to and beyond Fairfax Stone, the westernmost point in Maryland. Known as a well-managed rail system, it met its demise as a result of competition, the Great Depression, the rise of the trucking industry, and changing economic and demographic realities. By the mid-1970s most of its track mileage and rolling stock had been acquired by the Baltimore and Ohio Railroad. Within another decade, the old Western Maryland tracks had been abandoned.

Today, at least four scenic railways operate on what were once Western Maryland rails, including the popular Western Maryland Scenic Railway that runs from Cumberland to Frostburg. In other locations, the rights-of-way have been converted to rail trails, paved or graveled pathways perfect for walking or cycling. The Western Maryland Rail Trail (WMRT) is one of the best and longest of these, running almost 23 miles in the vicinity of Hancock, Maryland. Opened in sections between 1998 and 2004, the WMRT is paved with asphalt and runs within a stone's throw of the Potomac River for its entire length. In that distance, it begins just a mile from Fort Frederick State Park, with its historic restored fort dating from the French and Indian War. The town of Hancock, around halfway, provides opportunities for relaxation and refreshment and has a bike shop to service those inevitable breakdowns. Continuing west, the WMRT passes shale cliffs and limestone caves, each with an interesting geology and biota. The trail ends deep in the mountains near the edge of Green Ridge State Forest.

Trip Description

Many cyclists choose to begin their ride in Hancock, Maryland, with its easy access to I-70, plentiful parking, and amenities like food, drink, and bike repair. Unless you are able to set up a shuttle, you may find the full 46-mile round trip on the WMRT a bit too long for recreational purposes. Nevertheless, the full length of the WMRT will be described from its eastern terminus so as to provide an overview of the entire trail.

Mile zero of the WMRT is at the Big Pool Trailhead, where there is a portable restroom as well as parking for several dozen cars. But either before or after your ride, be sure to stop at Fort Frederick State Park, just a half mile east of Big Pool. The fort itself is an impressive structure made of the local sandstone. Built in 1756 as a defense against the depredations of Indians during the French and Indian War, the fort never saw violence. It was a prisoner-of-war camp during the Revolutionary War, and was merely garrisoned by Union troops during the Civil War. The fort was rebuilt during the Great Depression by the Civilian Conservation Corps and later became a Maryland state park. The grounds host re-enactors in period dress on occasions throughout the summer, and the sounds of black powder shoots echo off the surrounding hills several times a year.

Beginning your ride, the first point of interest is Big Pool itself, to the left. It's a natural pond that was used by canal boats on the adjacent C&O Canal as a resting and turning area. Today the pool is edged by wetlands, while water lilies, duckweed, and algae grow in the shallows. Great blue herons, green herons, and kingfishers are attracted to the small fish residing in the pool.

At mile one, Ernstville Road crosses the WMRT and provides a connection to the nearby C&O Canal towpath. This and several other access points permit a cyclist to pedal in one direction on the WMRT and return on the towpath, a way to experience both trails in one trip. Note that the C&O Canal towpath is mostly gravel, with some potholes and mud, making it a rougher ride that requires more exertion. Skinny-tired road bikes are not recommended on the towpath. (For more on the towpath, see the full description elsewhere in this book.)

The remaining eight miles between this point and Hancock are a bit less pleasant than a typical rail trail due to road noise from the

Iron gate on a cave

nearby I-70. Birds, however, seem unbothered by the roar of passing cars and trucks, and the adjacent floodplain forest hosts a rich variety of songbirds, including woodpeckers, chickadees, Northern cardinals, Carolina wrens, and white-breasted nuthatches year round, and catbirds, thrushes, and warblers in the warmer months.

The river town of Hancock parallels the WMRT for almost two miles, the trail passing by both junk-strewn backyards and well-kept businesses. There are many choices for a meal, a snack, or even overnight accommodations; a directory and map of the town is found along the trail at about mile 10.5. Cyclists will appreciate the full service bike shop located steps from the WMRT. A small park between the towpath and river makes a shady, pleasant place for a picnic or nap.

Heading west from Hancock, the WMRT becomes both more rural and quite scenic. Between mile 13 and 14, the trail cuts through the southern end of Roundtop Mountain, exposing several caves that are either visible from the trail or may be seen after just a short scramble uphill. These caves supplied limestone used in the manufacture of cement between 1838 and 1909. The caves have been sealed with iron gates that keep people out but allow several species of bats access to their hibernacula sites inside. Unfortunately, the fungal disease known as white nose syndrome has decimated bat populations here and in many other Maryland caves.

Downhill from the WMRT and visible from the C&O Canal towpath are the ruins of eight limestone kilns, all that is left of what was once a major manufacturing operation. Cement from this mill was used in the construction of the US Capitol and the Washington Monument.

Roundtop Mountain is just one of several north/south-trending ridges cut by the WMRT railbed, and shale cliffs border the trail for many of its remaining miles. Soil is a scarce commodity here, and the southern exposure makes these cliffs hot, dry places for plants. Look for purple asters, alumroot, columbine, and even prickly pear cacti on these cliffs.

The WMRT gains elevation coming out of Hancock, such that it is now about fifty feet higher than the nearby and generally parallel C&O Canal towpath. For cyclists interested in birds, this elevated position gives eye-level glimpses into the mid-canopy of trees lining the towpath. Birds like red-eyed vireos, yellow-billed cuckoos, Baltimore orioles, scarlet tanagers, and some warbler species all prefer the treetops, and so may be more easily viewed here.

This area of steep, parallel ridges marks the zone where two familiar and similar birds coexist: the black-capped chickadee and the Carolina chickadee. The black-capped is a bird of the north, common in New England and in the mountains of western Maryland, while the Carolina prefers more temperate climes to the south and in Maryland east of Hancock. These two species appear virtually identical to us humans, although their songs are different; the black-capped has a two-note song, while the Carolina has a four-note song. In areas where the two species overlap, hybridization may occur. Further confounding identification, each species may learn the other's song in this hybridization zone. Given these problems with identification of chickadees in this area, should you see this familiar bird, just call it a "chickadee" on your list and move on.

The final ridge on the WMRT is Sideling Hill, and the paved trail ends within a short distance of Sideling Hill Creek and its towpath aqueduct at the hamlet of Pearre. Although the old Western Maryland railbed continues west, further construction of the trail is unlikely because Indigo Tunnel houses several species of bats and has been sealed to prevent their disturbance.

Directions

From Baltimore or Washington, DC, take I-70 west past Hagerstown. Take exit 12, Route 56, Big Pool Road. Turn left on Route 56 and go less than a half mile to the well-marked trailhead parking lot.

Other Outdoor Recreational Opportunities Nearby

The C&O Canal towpath, adjacent to the WMRT, runs more than 100 miles in an eastward direction toward Washington, DC, and more than 70 miles west to Cumberland, Maryland. It is described in detail elsewhere in this book.

WHAT IS A SPECIES?

Chickadees are common and familiar birds that regularly visit backyard feeders. Two species exist in the eastern United States: Carolina chickadees and black-capped chickadees. To the casual observer, these two species appear identical. Fortunately, geography almost always permits identification; Carolinas are birds of the south, while black-caps are found in the north. The two species contact each other only in a narrow zone that runs latitudinally across the eastern United States and south along the spine of the Appalachian Mountains. The hills abutting the Western Maryland Rail Trail are a part of this contact zone. Here, the two species interbreed; as a result, as the noted ornithologist David Sibley writes, "chickadees are essentially unidentifiable."

All of this raises a question for naturalists, birders, and professional biologists: what is a species? The Biological Species Concept has been widely accepted and used for the last half century. It says that a species is a population of organisms that can actually or potentially interbreed with each other and produce viable offspring. Chickadees illustrate one problem with the Biological Species Concept; the two groups of chickadees clearly do interbreed in the places where both are found. The differences in

(continued)

physical appearance are subtle at best. Yet no one believes that Carolina and black-capped chickadees are one species.

Since about 2000, new techniques in DNA sequencing have made that process much faster and cheaper. As a result, it has been applied to the question of what constitutes a species. A portion of a gene is sequenced, then compared with similar data from another organism that may or may not be the same species. The degree of similarity in the sequence is then calculated and a statistical test is used to determine whether the two organisms are the same or different species.

In addition, DNA sequencing can give other kinds of information. For example, most humans alive today contain DNA sequences associated with Neanderthals. About 1 percent to 4 percent of our DNA, including sequences important for hair structure and the immune system, comes from Neanderthals. The data indicate that the two species of hominins interbred about 40,000 to 60,000 years ago.

DNA sequencing can also be used to study biological diversity, without defining which species are present. For example, if DNA is extracted from a soil sample, every living organism present in that soil sample contributes DNA. Then a complementary segment of DNA made in the laboratory, say for example the gene for cytochrome b, is added to the soil sample as a probe. It binds to any piece of DNA in the soil sample that codes for cytochrome b, no matter which species that cytochrome b sequence came from. All the probe/soil cytochrome b complexes are then isolated and each is sequenced. The number of species in the original soil sample can then be estimated from the number of different cytochrome b DNA sequences. Such experiments have shown that the number of bacterial species present in soil is far more than we ever imagined.

All this may sound esoteric and complex, but it is now fairly routine molecular biology. Black-capped and Carolina chickadees are different species based on molecular genetic data, despite their similarity in appearance and their ability to hybridize. But if you see a chickadee while riding the Western Maryland Rail Trail, you had best list it only as "chickadee species" in your field notes, and be content with that.

Great Allegheny Passage

Section: Cumberland to the Mason-Dixon Line

County: Allegany

Distance: 20.5 miles one way; 26 miles as described

Type: Multi-use recreational trail

Surface: Crushed limestone

Difficulty: Easy. Steadily rising toward Pennsylvania, but no hills

Hazards: Train tunnels

Highlights: Mountain scenery, steam trains, tunnels

More Information: Allegheny Trail Alliance, https://www.gaptrail.org; Western Maryland Scenic Railroad, https:// wmsr.com (301) 759-4400

Street Address: 13 Canal Street, Cumberland, Maryland 21502 (train station, Cumberland)

GPS Coordinates: 39.649518, 78.763627 (train station, Cumberland)

Cycle from Washington, DC, to Pittsburgh? It's a reality now that the Great Allegheny Passage (GAP Trail) is finished. With its origin in Cumberland, Maryland, and its terminus at the legendary Forks of the Ohio in Pittsburgh, the 150-mile long GAP Trail connects seamlessly with the C&O Canal towpath to create a route first envisioned by George Washington more than 250 years ago. Just over twenty miles of the GAP Trail exists in Maryland, following the railbed of the defunct Western Maryland Railway. While Maryland is the steepest section of the GAP Trail, the grade never exceeds 2 percent. Going uphill, that means you'll have to use a lower gear, and you'll notice the hill, but you are unlikely to get much out of breath or overly tired. Going downhill, the ride is easy, but friction with the crushed limestone path means you won't need your brakes, and you'll still have to do some pedaling at intervals.

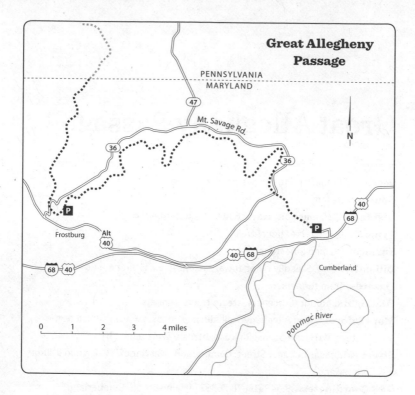

The Maryland portion of the GAP Trail shares the right-of-way with the Western Maryland Scenic Railroad (WMSR). The WMSR runs a seasonal daily excursion train along these tracks for fifteen miles between Cumberland and Frostburg. That means a train passes through the 914-foot Brush Tunnel twice a day. And on those days when their steam locomotive is running, you really do not want to be in that tunnel at the same time. Not only would it be unpleasant, but cinders and smoke would be a true hazard. Contact the WMSR for schedule information prior to your ride. North of Frostburg, the remaining five miles of trail in Maryland are quite pleasant, in a woodsy setting where there are few signs of humans beyond the rail corridor.

The GAP Trail continues north to Pittsburgh for another 125 miles beyond the Mason-Dixon line. That major portion of the trail is not described in this book, since it is in Pennsylvania. Nevertheless, the entire GAP Trail makes a wonderful multi-day cycling trip for those so inclined.

While one could (and many do) begin and end their GAP Trail trip in Cumberland, doing a 41-mile, out-and-back ride, I highly recommend combining your cycling experience with a ride on the Western Maryland Scenic Railroad. The baggage car is equipped to take bikes and does so on virtually every trip north. The experience is quite pleasant, and the views are exceptional, especially during fall color season in mid-October. Upon arrival in Frostburg, detrain with your bike, ride north five miles to the border (or beyond), and then enjoy an easy ride downhill to your starting point in Cumberland. The only drawback to this scheme is that the Railroad requires you to pay full fare, even though you are only riding the train one way.

Trip Description

Begin your ride from Cumberland, Maryland, just off I-68. There is ample parking in the city lot near the train station, where there are restrooms, drinking water, and food available. If you walk or ride underneath the I-68 bridge, be sure to check out Canal Place, which contains shops, restaurants, a national park visitor center, and, most importantly, a good bike shop for those last-minute needs and repairs. Canal Place marks mile 184.5 on the C&O Canal towpath and mile 0.0 of the Great Allegheny Passage. With your ticket in hand (purchased in advance from the WMSR website), follow their directions for loading your bike, and board the train for the pleasant and scenic ride to Frostburg.

Once at the Frostburg station, unload your bike from the train. If you wish to have lunch or see the sights of Frostburg, follow the crowds up the short but steep hill into town. To start your ride, take the path downhill to the GAP Trail, then ride north, uphill, to your left. This point marks mile 15 of the GAP Trail.

Within a short distance, Frostburg is left behind and the forests of the Allegheny Front surround you. As you climb higher, sugar maples assume a greater dominance, lending their stunning red and orange colors to the autumn palette. Sassafrass and red maple are also brilliantly colored fall trees and become more common as you near the Mason-Dixon line. If you hit the right day, there are few places in Maryland with better fall color than the GAP Trail.

Near mile 17.5, the trail enters Borden Tunnel, 957 feet long and unlighted. It can get quite dark in the middle of this tunnel;

a headlight or headlamp will be useful. The tunnel is more than a century old, having been built in 1911, abandoned by the railroad in 1975, and refurbished and reopened for the GAP Trail in 2004.

Another three miles of riding brings you to the Mason-Dixon line, the border between Pennsylvania and Maryland. It was surveyed between 1763 and 1767 by Charles Mason and Jeremiah Dixon to solve a border dispute between the two states. They set up stone markers at every mile of the 244 miles surveyed; each has a "P" on the north side and an "M" on the south side. A surprising number of these markers are still present after more than 250 years. At this point on the GAP Trail, a modern version of an old marker has been set up, a stone plinth about head-high. In addition, granite blocks pave the trail here in a long row; the effect is quite remarkable.

Since this book is about cycling Maryland trails, it's time to turn around for the ride back to Cumberland. Before doing so, however, well-conditioned riders may want to consider biking a few more miles north to experience two of the GAP Trail's most interesting features. At mile 22 is the Big Savage Tunnel, 3,300 feet in length with wonderful views of the surrounding countryside from just before its southern entry. Note that this tunnel is closed from mid-December to mid-April. At mile 23.5 is the Continental Divide, where falling rain may end up in either the Atlantic Ocean or the Gulf of Mexico. This also marks the high point on the GAP Trail at 2,390 feet above sea level. More significantly for the cyclist, trail's end at Cumberland is 1,765 feet lower in elevation. It's all downhill from here.

The return trip goes fast. From Frostburg south, the GAP Trail runs parallel to the rails of the Western Maryland Scenic Railroad, and so any sense that this is a remote wilderness trail is gone. Nevertheless, there are some interesting sights along the way. Perhaps the most photographed section of the GAP Trail is Helmstetter's Curve, at mile 5, where the railroad traverses a 180-degree sweeping arc. On days when the steam locomotive is running, expect to see many people with cameras jockeying for the best position trailside. One mile farther south, adjacent to the trail, is the Cumberland Bone Cave. In 1912, as railroad construction workers were blasting a cut in the rock, a fossil-filled cave was revealed. Scientists from the Smithsonian Museum in Washington, DC, spent the next four years excavating the cave, extracting many Pleistocene-era fossils. The full skeletons of a cave bear and a saber-toothed cat, almost 200,000 years old, are still on display today at the Smithsonian Natural History Museum.

The final two miles of the GAP Trail into Cumberland become increasingly urbanized, but there are some nice views of the Wills Creek valley below. Finally, the trail becomes paved and ends near the train station in Cumberland. The little Maryland mountain town has many opportunities for dining and relaxing within a few blocks of the train station, so enjoy.

Directions

Take I-70 west from either Baltimore or Washington, DC. Just past Hancock, Maryland, get on I-68. In Cumberland, at the bottom of the hill, take exit 43C. Turn left at the stop sign and go two blocks to Canal Place.

Other Outdoor Recreational Opportunities Nearby

A few miles east of Cumberland, right on I-68, is Rocky Gap State Park and Resort. In addition to the casino and hotel, there are some nice hiking trails, a lake, and a large campground.

AMERICAN WOODCOCKS

Unusual animals and their exotic mating behaviors can often be seen in documentary movies about nature, news service reports, and even You Tube videos, but one of the strangest performances takes place near dusk in March at a variety of locales around Maryland. The American woodcock is a chunky game bird with cryptic black, brown, gray, and white plumage, a long beak, short legs, and large eyes set high and back on the head. Its preferred habitat is wet woods with a mix of young trees and open damp meadows. But what sets woodcocks apart from other birds of forest and field is their mating "dance."

(continued)

As the March dusk settles in, both male and female wood-cocks arrive at a display site, called a lek. A male soon give his call, a nasal "peent" sound that carries surprisingly far. He then launches himself into the air, rising higher and higher, for a few hundred feet. At the apogee, he begins a chirping song that is supplemented by the rush of air past his wings, generating a whistling sound. His descent involves banks and turns, singing all the while, until he lands with an audible plop. Within a min-ute, he is usually off again on another display flight. All of these theatrics are to impress female woodcocks, who wait quietly and modestly on the lekking grounds. If sufficiently aroused, the female woodcock may accept the performer as a sperm donor; male woodcocks play no parental role with their offspring.

The now pregnant female, or hen, selects a nest site in brushy cover, creating a rudimentary scrape nest. On average, four eggs are laid and incubated for about three weeks. The chicks are precocial, leaving the nest almost immediately, and are usually probing for earthworms and insects with their long bills within days. They can make short flights in about two weeks and are completely independent by five weeks post hatching.

While the male woodcock flight displays are justifiably well known and appreciated among birders, woodcock foraging behavior is equally exotic, even amusing. The bird takes a step, rocks back and forth, takes another step, and so on. He resem-bles nothing so much as a chubby disco dancer perfecting a new strut. Scientists believe this foot-stamping behavior helps the bird locate invertebrate prey buried in the soil, much as robins listen for earthworms. The appearance, to us humans, is nothing short of humorous.

So when you want to get outside after a long winter, and if you're willing to brave the evening cold, head out to your local woodcock display site. Many nature centers offer one or two guided walks early each spring to these sites. You'll be amazed that so much is going on in the natural world, at times and in places you never even suspected. It's a wonderful world out there, so enjoy it!

Index

This index lists places, organisms, and concepts to which significant coverage is devoted in the text. It is not a listing of every occurrence of a word. Trip names are listed in boldface type. Italic page numbers refer to illustrations in the text. Illustrations in the photo gallery are indicated by *"color plate."*